MEN, MARTYRS AND
MOUNTEBANKS

MEN, MARTYRS
AND
MOUNTEBANKS

*Beverley Baxter's Inner Story of
Personalities and Events behind the War*

ARTHUR BEVERLEY BAXTER

Essay Index Reprint Series

BOOKS FOR LIBRARIES PRESS
FREEPORT, NEW YORK

First Published 1940
Reprinted 1970

STANDARD BOOK NUMBER:
8369-1446-5

LIBRARY OF CONGRESS CATALOG CARD NUMBER:
73-104992

PRINTED IN THE UNITED STATES OF AMERICA

To my son Clive in the hope that when he reaches man's estate there will be fewer Martyrs and Mountebanks than to-day

CONTENTS

CHAPTER		PAGE
I.	THE INCREDIBLE FORTY-EIGHT HOURS	9
II.	CAUSE AND EFFECT	25
III.	THE TWO GERMANYS	40
IV.	AT THE GERMAN EMBASSY	56
V.	AN EMPIRE ANSWERS	70
VI.	THE GREAT NEUTRAL	88
VII.	MOONLIGHT OVER BUCHAREST	103
VIII.	STALIN PLAYS HIS HAND	113
IX.	VISITOR TO PARIS	121
X.	THE JUNIOR PARTNER	130
XI.	POLONAISE MILITAIRE	142
XII.	BLACK-OUT	149
XIII.	THE RIDDLE OF THE AIR	161
XIV.	GENTLEMEN V. GOEBBELS	172
XV.	THE NEW CONTEMPTIBLES	186
XVI.	THE PEACE OFFENSIVE	203
XVII.	STRANGE WAR	240
XVIII.	CHURCHILL AND THE FLEET	251
XIX.	EUROPE YESTERDAY, TO-DAY AND TO-MORROW	265
XX.	PATIENCE EXHAUSTED	278

MEN, MARTYRS AND MOUNTEBANKS

Chapter I

The Incredible Forty-eight Hours

AT 11 O'CLOCK ON SUNDAY MORNING, SEPtember 3rd, 1939, Great Britain was at war with Germany.

There was lovely weather. Never have the countryside and the sea called more strongly to the town dweller. But there was no exodus on that day. The nation was waiting for the news which it felt had become inevitable.

At 11.15 Mr. Chamberlain spoke on the radio.

He told us that we were at war. His voice was firm, but sad. For him it was the end of a dream. When he had finished there was a pause, and then a gramophone record was played, giving us the National Anthem. There was another pause. In businesslike tones the B.B.C. announcer began to give us the first of the hundreds of regulations which were to be fastened upon the British people. One listened with mixed thoughts and dulled emotions. There was little time to think and little time to feel.

For the first time Britain was prepared for a war and the edicts of Whitehall were upon us.

"That is the end of the announcements"—our wireless sets were silenced.

Each of us has his own memory of that moment. Some, like myself, had a rendezvous at Westminster at twelve noon to hear what we had already heard.

High up, in the almost Mediterranean sky, the grotesque defence balloons were gleaming like distorted, silver boxing gloves. There was no one on the streets. There was not a sound of a single motor car.

At that moment a great chromatic wail rising over London, rose and fell, and rose and fell. The air raid warning which, once or twice, we had heard in rehearsals finding its voice over the teeming noises of the town, now had the air to itself.

The Germans were coming.

At any minute now, that which we had all foreseen would come to pass.

Thank God the children had gone away. Thank God for John Anderson, thank God for Hore-Belisha and his anti-aircraft guns. Now we were to see the madman's attempt to humble mighty London in the dust.

I must confess to a sneaking admiration at that moment of the Nazi Government. Our ultimatum had expired at eleven o'clock; now, barely half an hour later, 5,000 machines were bringing their answer. Let us give credit where it is due. There is something about those Germans. . . .

The ghastly wail went on. Never did human ingenuity so fasten the spirit of horror to a mechanical device. But there was that rendezvous at Westminster. It was an interesting point. Were His Majesty's legislators to assemble in the Palace of Westminster in obedience to Mr. Speaker's summons, or were they to

The Incredible Forty-eight Hours

take cover in obedience to the orders of Sir John Anderson?

The drive to the Houses of Parliament was an interesting experience. Such traffic as there was had been drawn up to the side of the roads and occupants were going to ground. Air raid wardens with their steel helmets beckoned to us like the maiden who tried to stop the young man climbing the mountain with his banner of 'Excelsior'. The army of A.R.P. workers, men and women, were at their posts in every section of the country. They were ready to go into the streets, into the very flames of hell to carry out the duties to which they had pledged themselves. Nurses stood by their cots and amateur firemen waited for their orders.

The House of Commons met at 12. There was a Speaker's procession and the ritual of prayers. They gave a secure sense of permanence to a world that was collapsing at our feet.

Those who read these words will expect to be told that the scene was intensely dramatic. That faces were flushed with excitement and that voices trembled with emotion when they spoke.

Instead of that there was an almost complete absence of emotion. I cannot explain it. Perhaps the events of the past few months with their steadily developing inevitability of war, perhaps the things which had happened in the House in the previous forty-eight hours—it is hard to say. We knew that we were witnessing a great historic scene and yet the element of drama seemed curiously missing. Perhaps it was because there was no passionate conflict of opinion, probably it was the lack of surprise. Then again the broadcast announcement of the Prime Minister had already told us the news. To some extent we were like mummers performing in a play which the audience had already seen. There was incongruity to the eye, however. Half a dozen of the younger Members were in uniform. One M.P., a mere boy in appearance, was booted and spurred and wore the badges of a Colonel. Another, only a year or two older, had come in uniform from his Air Squadron. A third and older M.P. was dressed as a Lance-Corporal.

Nor was there any sense of excitement in the gallery. Even the Ambassadors appeared rather like a Board of Directors attending the liquidation of a business that had once promised well.

M. Corbin of France looked exactly the same as on any similar occasion in the past two years. His fine, pale face is utterly impassive, his delicate hands are always still. No one could ever read his thoughts. Nor were they on view that morning. Beside him sat Count Raczynski, the Polish Ambassador. The last time I had seen him was at a dinner party given in July at the American Embassy in honour of Queen Mary. Count Raczynski had just returned from Poland. His gaiety was delightful and his wit was sparkling. Life was an adventure to him and the gathering shadows could not depress his spirit. Now, in the gallery of the House of Commons, his face was grim. While other nations were moving towards war with careful steps, his countrymen were reeling back from an attack that gave them no chance to rally. Near to him sat Mr. Joseph Kennedy, the American Ambassador. He looked so unlike himself, so much older,

The Incredible Forty-eight Hours

that for a moment I could not believe that this was the man who had made so profound an inroad into the affections of the British people. Of all the faces there, his was the one which most clearly showed the marks of suffering. I did not know then that a few minutes before he had been to Downing Street to see the Prime Minister. Mr. Chamberlain received him alone in the Cabinet room. They shook hands. They said the conventional things and then both men could keep up the pretence no longer. Openly and unashamedly they wept.

Somewhere in the gallery of the Diplomatic Corps there was poor little Maisky, the Russian Ambassador, seeming to have shrunk a little, like his country's reputation. For a few brief months while the flirtation of Russia and the Allies had been on, M. Maisky had experienced something of the exhilaration of Cinderella. He had been taken from the kitchen to be the Princess at the ball. Flattery had been poured upon him and Russia had been praised as a civilizing force. At the gala performance at Covent Garden given by H.M. the King for the French President, little Maisky stood in the very centre of the front of the diplomats' box and bestowed his smile upon the entire scene. Now he was an outcast again, privileged to enter the gallery of the House, but no longer one of the sacred brethren. Russia had sold the pass, and Russia's Ambassador reverted to his permanent position of diplomatic outsider.

Directly behind the clock sat the Duke of Kent and the Duke of Gloucester. Their faces were earnest but impassive as they gazed down upon the elected representatives of the people.

Men, Martyrs and Mountebanks

The Prime Minister was cheered when he entered. He looked utterly haggard and his hands shook as he fingered the notes which were to be the basis of his speech. Opposite him sat Lloyd George, the architect of victory in the last war. Beside him on the Government Front Bench was Sir John Simon, who had sat in the same place when Sir Edward Grey, twenty-five years ago, had described the ultimatum to Germany. On the corner seat below the gangway sat Winston Churchill, who had been First Lord of the Admiralty in 1914 and who was feeling the salt spray of the ocean upon his face again. At last he was certain that he would be called back to office and the Navy.

Chamberlain rose to speak.

I wondered how he would carry himself because he had been the centre, on the previous night, of one of the most painful scenes in the history of the Commons.

It must be recalled that for thirty-six hours previous to the Saturday, Poland had been at war with Germany—and it must be remembered that our promise was to go immediately to her assistance. Mr. Chamberlain had said that he would make his pronouncement to the House some time on the Saturday afternoon. We met on that anxious day, but at the usual time. For a while we passed the various measures of autocracy which the Government were demanding. There was a rumour that the Prime Minister would not speak until 6 o'clock. When 6 o'clock came he had not appeared, and so we adjourned until 7. Needless to say, the smoke-room and the lobbies were miniature parliaments in themselves. There was a torrent of talk. Fierce arguments and grave doubts. But in every breast there was a gnawing anxiety

The Incredible Forty-eight Hours

about our guarantee to Poland. We had promised to act at once and we were still not at war. We trooped back to the darkened chamber. Mr. Chamberlain rose to speak.

Because of the sensation that followed, I think it only just to put on record the exact words of the Prime Minister.

"Sir Nevile Henderson was received by Herr von Ribbentrop at half-past nine last night, and he delivered the warning message which was read to the House yesterday. Herr von Ribbentrop replied that he must submit the communication to the German Chancellor. Our Ambassador declared his readiness to receive the Chancellor's reply. Up to the present no reply has been received.

"It may be that the delay is caused by consideration of a proposal which, meanwhile, has been put forward by the Italian Government, that hostilities should cease and that there should then immediately be a conference between the five Powers, Great Britain, France, Poland, Germany and Italy. While appreciating the efforts of the Italian Government, His Majesty's Government, for their part, would find it impossible to take part in a conference while Poland is being subjected to invasion, her towns are under bombardment and Danzig is being made the subject of a unilateral settlement by force. His Majesty's Government will, as stated yesterday, be bound to take action unless the German forces are withdrawn from Polish territory. They are in communication with the French Government as to the limit of time within which it would be necessary for the British and French Governments to know whether the German Government were prepared to effect such a withdrawal. If the German Government should agree to withdraw their forces then His Majesty's Government would be willing to regard the position as being the same as it was before the German forces crossed the Polish frontier. That is to say, the way would be open to discussion between the German and Polish Governments on the matters at issue between them, on the understanding that the settlement arrived at was one that safeguarded the vital interests of Poland and was secured by an international guarantee. If the German and Polish Governments wished that other Powers should be associated with them in the discussion, His Majesty's Government for their part would be willing to agree.

"There is one other matter to which allusion should be made in order that the present situation may be perfectly clear. Yesterday Herr Förster who, on 23rd August, had, in contravention of the Danzig constitution, become the head of the State, decreed the incorporation of Danzig in the Reich and the dissolution of the Constitution. Herr Hitler was asked to give effect to this decree by German law. At a meeting of the Reichstag yesterday morning a law was passed for the reunion of Danzig with the Reich. The international status of Danzig as a Free City is established by a treaty of which His Majesty's Government are a signatory, and the Free City was placed under the protection of the League of Nations. The rights given to Poland in Danzig by treaty are defined and confirmed by agreement concluded between Danzig and Poland. The action taken by the Danzig authorities and the Reichstag yesterday is the final step in the unilateral repudiation of these international instruments, which could only be modified by negotiation. His Majesty's Government do not, therefore, recognize either the validity of the grounds on which the action of the Danzig authorities was based, the validity of this action itself, or of the effect given to it by the German Government."

The Incredible Forty-eight Hours

Reading it now in the calmness of time, one may perhaps wonder why this speech should have loosed such a torrent of resentment in almost every part of the House. Perhaps it can be explained by stating that, absorbed as he was in the problem at hand, the Prime Minister utterly failed to foresee the mood of the Members.

The day before he had denounced Hitler and arraigned him before the bar of history. What is more, he had sent a note to the German Government demanding an immediate reply. Thirty-six hours had passed. Thirty-six hours of waiting on our part and thirty-six hours of death and destruction in Poland. We did not know that there was a last desperate chance of peace and that Chamberlain was holding back the hands of the clock to keep it from striking. All we heard were his uninspired, legalistic, meticulous words. No expression of sympathy for the Poles, no passionate denunciation of Hitler, not one tribute to the spirit of France. Many of us who had believed, and still believe, that the debt of civilisation to Chamberlain can never be paid, were sick at heart at the utter inadequacy of his speech. Only two explanations seemed possible to us. Either we were entering into a deal with the murderer of Poland, or France was hesitating to honour her pledge to us. If such thought seemed unworthy now, or hysterical, remember the tense atmosphere of the scene. Remember, too, the shame we all were feeling that Poland was at war, that France and ourselves, her guarantors, were at peace.

There were no cheers when Mr. Chamberlain sat down. Instead, there was an angry murmur that grew louder and louder as Mr. Greenwood, the acting Leader of the Opposition, rose to speak.

Suddenly, Colonel Amery, from the Government back benches, leaned forward. "Speak for England," he cried. The words cut the air like a knife. A dozen Tory voices took up the cry. "Speak for England. Speak for England. Speak for England."

Chamberlain went white. For a moment I thought he might collapse. It was as if he had been struck a blow between the eyes. Greenwood stood silent and flushed, but his thoughts must have been tempestuous. What a situation for him, the Labour Leader, that he had been asked to voice the true spirit of the nation!

To his credit, he refused to capitalize this emotional outburst. For one thing, the Prime Minister had previously explained to him the situation of Mussolini's intervention and to that extent Greenwood was party to the manœuvre. Even so, he could have added cruelly to the humiliation of the Premier. Instead, he spoke like a statesman, for there is an element of greatness in this man Greenwood. Pointing to Chamberlain, he said: "Which of you would want the responsibility that is on his shoulders at this hour?"

When he had finished, the Prime Minister asked for permission to speak again. In his state of agitation, he said: "I should be horrified if the House thought for one moment that the statement that I have made to them betrayed the slightest weakening either of this Government or of the French Government in the attitude which we have already taken up. . . . I understand that the French Cabinet is in session at this moment, and I feel certain that I can make a statement to the House of a definite character

The Incredible Forty-eight Hours

to-morrow when the House meets again. I am the last man to neglect any opportunity which I consider affords a serious chance of avoiding the great catastrophe of war even at the last moment, but I confess that, in the present case, I should have to be convinced of the good faith of the other side, in any action they took, before I could regard the proposition which has been made as one to which we could expect a reasonable chance of a successful issue. I anticipate that there is only one answer I shall be able to give to the House to-morrow. I hope that the issue will be brought to a close at the earliest possible moment so that we may know where we are, and I trust that the House, realizing the position which I have tried to put before it, will believe me that I speak in complete good faith and will not prolong the discussion which, perhaps, might make our position more embarrassing than it is."

Looking back, I can feel the sympathy now which was impossible to summon at that moment. The French were moving their divisions into position and saw no advantage in declaring war so long as the Germans would allow them to complete their disposition of troops. It was the French mind treating the crisis with complete calm.

Chamberlain knew all this. There was no weakening of purpose on his part. There was just an inadequacy of expression which utterly failed to take into account the feelings of the House.

A few hours later, at midnight, I was making my way along the empty Strand, where sandbags were piled against the buildings. It was pitch-black save for the tiny illuminated crosses that have replaced the traffic lights. Suddenly a thunderstorm broke. Wild flashes of lightning lit up the eerie scene. The thunder crashed over our heads. There was tragedy in the air—stark, ghastly tragedy. It is written that on the day of the Crucifixion the skies were like that.

Perhaps with such a prelude it was small wonder that when the House met on Sunday there was a feeling of calm despite the sirens that continued to howl outside. We were at war. We could look the world in the face. The sense of shame that had branded us the previous day was no longer there.

When Mr. Chamberlain rose to speak he was given a deep-throated cheer as if to tell him that all was forgiven.

His opening words dealt not with the war but with what had happened in the House the night before:

> "When I spoke last night to the House I could not but be aware that in some parts of the House there were doubts and some bewilderment as to whether there had been any weakening, hesitation or vacillation on the part of His Majesty's Government. In the circumstances, I make no reproach, for if I had been in the same position as hon. Members not sitting on this Bench, and not in possession of all the information which we have, I should very likely have felt the same."

It was the *amende honorable*, and the House, which is as swift in magnanimity as it is in resentment, consigned the whole affair to the archives of history.

Mr. Chamberlain then went on to say:

> "The statement which I have to make this morning will show that there were no grounds for doubt. We

were in consultation all day yesterday with the French Government and we felt that the intensified action which the Germans were taking against Poland allowed no delay in making our own position clear. Accordingly, we decided to send to our Ambassador in Berlin instructions which he was to hand at 9 o'clock this morning to the German Foreign Secretary, and which read as follows:

" 'Sir,

" 'In the communication which I had the honour to make to you on the 1st September, I informed you, on the instructions of His Majesty's Principal Secretary of State for Foreign Affairs, that unless the German Government were prepared to give His Majesty's Government in the United Kingdom satisfactory assurance that the German Government had suspended all aggressive action against Poland and were prepared promptly to withdraw their forces from Polish territory, His Majesty's Government in the United Kingdom would, without hesitation, fulfil their obligations to Poland.

" 'Although this communication was made more than twenty-four hours ago, no reply has been received but German attacks upon Poland have been continued and intensified. I have accordingly the honour to inform you that, unless not later than 11 a.m. British Summer Time, to-day 3rd September, satisfactory assurances to the above effect have been given by the German Government and have reached His Majesty's Government in London, a state of war will exist between the two countries as from that hour.'

"That was the final Note. No such undertaking was received by the time stipulated, and, consequently, this country is at war with Germany. I am in a position to inform the House that, according to arrangements made between the British and French Governments, the French Ambassador in Berlin is at this moment making a similar *démarche*, accompanied also by a definite time limit. The House has already been made aware of our plans. As I said the other day, we are ready.

"This is a sad day for all of us, and to none is it sadder than to me. Everything that I have worked for, everything that I have hoped for, everything that I have believed in during my public life, has crashed into ruins. There is only one thing left for me to do ; that is, to devote what strength and powers I have to forwarding the victory of the cause for which we have to sacrifice so much. I cannot tell what part I may be allowed to play myself; I trust I may live to see the day when Hitlerism has been destroyed and a liberated Europe has been re-established."

When he sat down a sympathetic cheer was given to him from the whole House. Followers, doubters and critics—all of us realized the personal tragedy of the Premier who had worked so hard for peace.

The official spokesmen of the Opposition Labour and Liberal parties followed. Their speeches showed that Parliament, like the country, was absolutely united.

At this point in the proceedings the air raid warnings stopped.

The short blast of police whistles sounded through the lobbies. Whatever was going to happen had not happened—at least in London.

Mr. Churchill rose. The House accorded him a generous and enthusiastic reception. The man of climax and anti-climax had proved to be right in his warnings to the nation. It is strange now to recall that just as Churchill was on the eve of an immense wave of popularity and tremendous success both in the House and in the country, on that morning he should have fallen far below his standard. The reason was that he had too carefully prepared his speech. If he had come there content to judge the atmosphere of the House, his would have been a voice to stir our emotions from their lethargy.

Instead he spoke with such epic style that it smacked of the professional orator, the too conscientious pupil of Pericles. The language was too colourful, the sentiment too significant, the style too momentous. Perhaps history will record his efforts that morning as a triumph. We in the House took a different view.

On the other hand, Mr. Lloyd George could not have been better.

For the last three or four years he has been faced on nearly every occasion with a bitter and hostile House of Commons. There was hardly a speech which he had made which had not brought recrimination upon his patriarchal head. But when he spoke on that Sunday morning we suddenly saw the incarnation of victory, the man who had led us with such gay and persistent courage through the dark days of the last war. A great cheer swept the Chamber. It must have sounded sweet music to his ears. Without a note and with a compelling simplicity he pledged his support to the Prime Minister and offered to help in any capacity no matter how humble. His words are worth recording :

"I am one of those who, with hon. and right hon. Friends on this side of the House, have from time to time challenged the handling of foreign affairs by the Government, but this is a different matter. The Government are now confronted with the latest, but I am afraid not the last, of a series of acts of brigandage by a very formidable military Power, which if they are left unchallenged will undermine the whole foundations of civilization throughout the world. The Government could do no other than what they have done. I am one out of tens of millions in this country who will back any Government that is in power in fighting this struggle through, in however humble a capacity we may be called upon to render service to our country. I have been through this before, and there is only one word I want to say about that. We had very bad moments, moments when brave men were rather quailing and doubting, but the nation was firm right through, from beginning to end. One thing that struck me then was that it was in moments of disaster, and in some of the worst disasters with which we were confronted in the War, that I found the greatest union among all classes, the greatest disappearance of discontent and disaffection, and of the grabbing for rights and privileges. The nation closed its ranks then. By that means we went through right to the end, and after four and a half years, terrible years, we won a victory for right. We will do it again."

Nothing could have better suited the spirit of the occasion or the mood of the House.

A young Tory M.P. followed the old Welshman. He made a recruiting-speech. The House began to empty.

Walking across Palace Yard with a colleague, I made the obvious remark that "we had seen history in the making."

"Do you know," he said, "I am getting a little tired of history, we have had so much of it."

Thus did the British Parliament declare the nation to be at war.

Chapter II

Cause and Effect

To-day is the parent of to-morrow. The crime of the second world war is not due to one man alone, or one nation. Hitler stands arraigned for all time as the chief criminal but he could not have brought this catastrophe upon the world simply by the malevolent darkness of his mind. Nor could the German passion to enslave and be enslaved have plunged Europe unaided again into dreadful, inhuman war.

It has been said that the great struggles of the world are not between Right and Wrong. In such struggles the issue is too clear. The great wars between nations—as the great differences between individuals —are caused by the struggle between the Right and the Partially Right.

But all lessons of history are learned slowly.

For example, when the fighting ceases after a long, protracted conflict, the victor is tired. The winning nation is like a boxer who has put all his strength into a knock-out blow and has nothing more to give, no more resources on which to call.

On November 11th, 1918, the streets of London went wild with the jubilation and relief of a people from whom the tragedy of war was passing. There was a universal desire almost at once to get back to what had gone before. It was a fatal delusion. We should have realized then what we have so bitterly learned since—that the world which had existed before 1914 was dead.

On August Bank Holiday, 1914, Lancashire played Yorkshire at Old Trafford, Surrey played Notts at the Oval, and there was the usual holiday meeting at Sandown Park. All these things were suspended during the war.

Twenty-five years later, on August Bank Holiday, 1939, Lancashire played Yorkshire at Old Trafford, Surrey played Notts at the Oval, and there was the usual Bank Holiday meeting at Sandown Park.

No one will be foolish enough to condemn any of these things in themselves except that they were symptomatic of the whole psychology of Great Britain. The cry was "Back, back, back. . . ." We did not know that the old world died and a new one was born in the agony of Flanders.

If for no other reason a victorious nation must look ahead because its beaten adversary dare not look back. The loser has its eyes fastened on the future. Crushed, disillusioned, beaten in the field, impoverished at home, yet there is always a terrific power of resurgence in a defeated nation which is forgotten by the victors in the moment of triumph.

The abdication of King Edward VIII was not an isolated incident in itself. Rather was it the climax of a spirit of abdication which went slowly through British life until it culminated in the unhappy moment when a much loved British king, with all his vast potentialities of service to mankind, chose to lay down his crown.

There was a new medium of entertainment called the film. The control of the screen was almost

Cause and Effect

as important to Britain as the control of the seas.

Of all countries, we needed most to put into films the story of Britain's life, the story of her philosophy and the story of her greatness.

Instead, we abdicated to Hollywood.

In the theatre there was a flutter of life after the war. It seemed for a moment as if a new spirit might bring fresh glories to the English drama. That flicker proved to be a light that failed. Britain's playwrights could not bring themselves to write of the fresh new world which was hammering at the gates. In the realm of literature the giants of the late 'nineties still held the field. Wells, Bennett, Galsworthy, Shaw, Hardy—no new figure rose to challenge their place and they were growing tired—except Bernard Shaw, whose only sign of age was to decline from the passionate jester to the ironic philosopher.

Again it was left to America for her novelists to find a new vitality and an affinity with the spirit of the age. The result was crude and often repellent, but there was life in it.

Only in the realm of music was there a real advance in Britain. The younger composers obviously found inspiration in the post-war world. Of all the younger schools of composition they were infinitely the best. Since, however, the popular British Press pays no attention to music and the State gives no assistance it must remain a bankrupt of the arts. Indifference did its best to quench the genius which had arisen.

Even in the realm of religion it seemed as if the Church itself had lost its divine spark of inspiration. New movements such as the Oxford Group sprang up, just as in politics there were mushroom growths like Sir Oswald Mosley's campaign, born out of the inertia and lack of leadership which characterized life in these islands.

In the affairs of Empire there was a heartbreak recession of the spirit. The feeling grew that if we paid no attention to our possessions the rest of the world might not notice that we had them. For a short time Lord Beaverbrook bravely raised a banner with the strange device of 'Empire Free Trade', and tried to carry the campaign of Joseph Chamberlain once more through the country. Had it been better organized, and had there not been a natural distrust of what was called 'newspaper dictation' that movement might have become one of the most powerful forces in politics. As it was, it came to an end, leaving Great Britain, the heart of the Empire, without a single political figure whose life was dedicated to the building up of the British Commonwealth of Nations.

So far I have put the bad side of the case and we would be less than honest if we failed to realize its importance. But there were other forces at work with the British people which were commendable and which seemed to offer a definite advance in civilized standards.

America had created, abandoned and bequeathed to us the League of Nations. It was a magnificent conception, worthy of the greatest traditions of the American people. It promised the rule of justice and the law of arbitration as opposed to the settlement of disputes by war. With America permanently at the council table it must have become a reality. When the politicians of Washington, however, decided that the defeat of Woodrow Wilson was more important than the future of civilization, it left the League little more than a combination of nations headed by the victorious powers whose chief purpose was to carry out the harsh and unimaginative clauses of the Treaty of Versailles.

There was, too, that deceptive phrase, 'collective security.' It appealed alike to the idealist and to the realist.

The idealist saw in it a better order of things where the only sword would be that which was held in the hand of Justice.

The realist saw in it a world-wide protection for the existence and continuation of the British Empire.

The corollary was inevitable—disarmament. And someone had to give the lead.

Thus the world saw Great Britain, the head of a scattered Empire which sprawled the seven seas, throwing away the arms by which she had always maintained the safety of her possessions. Owning the strongest Air Force in existence at the end of the war, she let her flying armada dwindle to nothing. Even the Navy was lowered to the level of the first-line defence for a second-rate power.

In partial justification of that, one must recall that the defence experts gave it as their opinion in 1918 that there could be no large scale war involving Britain for ten years. This was a sensible view borne out by events. Unfortunately though, not only did Britain give the lead in disarmament, but she allowed to go into decline the very industries which would have to produce guns and ammunition if emergency called once more.

Men, Martyrs and Mountebanks

There was wide vision in the policy of unilateral disarmament, but it took insufficient account of the realities.

While economic injustices remain, men will seek to remedy them by force. And, as long as economic injustices remain, careerists will see in the misery of the people their chance of fame and power.

Except for a brief period when Mr. Lloyd George and Mr. Bonar Law were the heads of the Government, Great Britain had as its Premier one of two poets—Mr. Ramsay MacDonald or Mr. Stanley Baldwin. Both were men of the highest integrity and character.

Both, in the best sense, were world citizens. Both were mystics, dreamers; homely folk; gentle at heart and lovers of books. One smoked a pipe and the other spent his holidays watching his kettle simmer on the kitchen stove at Lossiemouth.

In the harsh development of events, the names of Baldwin and MacDonald have come under bitter criticism. Yet in their own way they offered a better civilization to mankind and deepened the basic humanitarianism of British life. That, at least, should be remembered as partial mitigation.

Nor was their foreign policy an easy thing to administer. The withdrawal of America had left a frightful responsibility to Britain. France, twice invaded in the memory of living men, was determined to keep Germany in a position where a third invasion would be impossible. If it was wrong, who can blame her?

It is true that M. Briand sought to replace enmity with friendship and to heal the scars of war with the balm of mutual trust. He failed but it was a glorious failure.

British policy was caught between cross currents, We wanted to keep faith with France. But we refused to be a partner in the severity of her realism towards Germany. We wanted to help Germany to rise. But we dared not seem to be planning a renewed and powerful Teutonic State to offset the will of France. Thus we would not support the French march into the Ruhr. Nor, on the other hand, did we give to Bruening or Stresemann the whole-hearted assistance which might have made the German Republic an instrument for good in the world.

As far as is possible in the pursuit of those half-hearted policies, we did many things for Germany. Of all the lies which Hitler has told his people, nothing is more monstrous than to say that Britain refused the hand of succour to prostrate Germany.

When the commercial Anschluss between Austria and Germany was first proposed in 1931 we not only supported it but voted for it at the Hague.

When President Hoover, anxious to lighten the burdens of Europe, suggested that we should forgive Germany her reparations, we did so—although leaving our own debt to America still in existence. We withdrew our army of occupation long before the time set down. We secured the entry of Germany into the League of Nations against opposition from many quarters. We signed a naval pact, thus officially recognizing that Germany had emerged from the position of a prisoner of war and had the right to negotiate matters for her own defence. The list could be added to over and over again. Inadequate and uninspired as her policy may have been, Great Britain did much to alleviate the suffering of the German Republic.

I have already said that the defence experts of Great Britain declared in 1918 that there would be no war for us for ten years. At the end of that period the European military situation was reviewed annually. In other words there was a year to year policy. As was to be expected the soldiers warned the successive British Governments that our forces were inadequate. These warnings, however, made no deep impression. After all, what kind of a military expert would it be who would not say that he wanted more of everything? So politicians continued to live in dreamland and to believe that a sky which was so clear would never again produce lightning. They had forgotten how swiftly clouds can gather.

War threatened Britain in 1931 when Japan invaded Manchuria. The same threat came when Italy cast lustful eyes towards Abyssinia. It came again when Hitler marched his troops into the Rhineland. To a lesser extent there was a chance of war when Hitler, breaking his word, sent his divisions into Austria, but the culmination came in September 1938 when the Third Reich determined to break up the little Republic of Czechoslovakia.

I suppose as long as men discuss politics there will be fierce arguments as to the wisdom or unwisdom of Britain's action at the time of the Abyssinian affair. Viscount Cecil and his followers declare that what should have been a death blow for Italian Fascism, turned out instead to be a death blow for the League of Nations.

Cause and Effect

Certainly, the spectacle of Italy defying Great Britain, France, Turkey, Yugo-Slavia, Czechoslovakia and the remaining signatories of the Covenant is not without humour. Like so many Britons I had the greatest love for Italy and her charming people. But even if every Italian had fought like an ancient Roman she must still have met disaster at an early stage in the campaign. Firm action on our part might have given to the League that breath of life which would have brought colour to its palsied skin and set its heart beating once more.

But, it must be repeated, not only is to-day the parent of to-morrow, but yesterday is the parent of to-day.

We had angered Japan without restraining her in 1931. European war with Italy might have created Japan's opportunity in the far East. A cautious policy at that time may have been wrong, but at least it had good arguments on its side.

There were other forces at work as well.

France had but recently concluded a treaty of friendship with Italy. The French attempt to draw a *cordon sanitaire* about Germany was, if not complete, at least enormously strengthened by the adhesion of the Italian nation. Above all things the French do not indulge in self-deception. As the creators of a colonial empire they did not see why they themselves or Great Britain should suddenly decide to die in defence of a backward civilization such as that enjoyed by the Abyssinians.

"We have only one enemy," said France, "Europe has only one enemy—why drive Italy into Germany's hands?"

Men, Martyrs and Mountebanks

The Quai d'Orsay did not attempt to dissemble. The French Government, while acknowledging the League as an instrument of idealism, regarded it primarily as a restraining hand on the ambitions of Germany.

As a result London learned that if the British fleet became involved in the Mediterranean it would be unwise to expect assistance from French warships.

All this, of course, might have been changed if once the guns had begun to speak, but that must always remain a matter for conjecture and debate.

At any rate, Britain decided not to send her ships or her young men against Italy. Mussolini had experienced his greatest triumph—the League its greatest disaster. In Berlin a new resolution swept through the veins of the Nazi leaders. Mussolini had shown them that the law of force was irresistible. The Nazis looked towards the future with eyes that refused to recognize any horizon. At the death of a king, a new one rises. At the death of the League, the Axis was born.

Manchuria was the forerunner of Abyssinia. After Abyssinia the next step was inevitable—the march into the Rhineland. Here again, conjecture and argument must hold the field until history pronounces its verdict. The sentimental case for Germany marching into her own territory was one that appealed to every Englishman. He said to himself that if we had been defeated and Sussex disarmed, we would have counted the days until that lovely county was once more brought under the military protection of the whole nation.

Cause and Effect

The French took a different view. To them the method was everything.

For the first time Hitler had used armed troops to right the Treaty of Versailles. The French Generals contended that the rifle can only be answered by the rifle, and that the march of German troops into the Rhineland should have been met by the march of France's army.

The League met in alarm in London. I remember so well the scene at St. James's Palace when M. van Zeeland in his beautiful French warned his hearers of the menace to the little nations that this move had created.

M. Litvinoff, like a Russianized Mr. Pickwick, took careful notes and smiled on everyone.

Anthony Eden, the Sir Galahad of world affairs, moved from delegate to delegate with the eyes of everyone upon him.

As far as I remember, nothing was decided. At any rate the League adjourned—which was one of the characteristics of that organization.

The fate of Europe still hung in the balance.

Talk dissipated the instinct for action. Against the advice of his Generals, Hitler had triumphed. His position in the Reich was greater than ever and his shadow fell upon the entire Continent.

I would not like to have had it in my power at the moment of any of those crises to say what we should do. Perhaps the soundest thing would have been to agree with the French and say: "Force must be met by force, threat by threat." At any rate the Rhineland was occupied and the fierce beam of Nazi ambition turned slowly towards Austria.

Men, Martyrs and Mountebanks

In considering those tangible and intangible things which led to the present war, even Austria played its part.

If only Dollfuss had made terms with the workers; if only Schuschnigg had not rebuffed the young King Otto; a united Austria might have withstood the German advance and by doing so have brought other nations to its rescue.

Unfortunately the bombardment of the workers' flats in Vienna had exposed the lovely city on the Danube to its ultimate fate.

Of all the places which have gone down before the Nazi aggression none makes such a nostalgic appeal as Vienna. Those of us who saw it shortly after the German invasion will not soon forget the experience.

Vienna was like a beautiful woman, perhaps a little faded, but still elegant, perhaps with more charm than character. In the madness of moonlight she had taken a lover to her arms and at daylight had found herself embraced by a monster.

For years Austrian Nazism had been forced to live underground. Now it reared its head in all its sadistic ugliness. Everywhere one went, everywhere one turned, stories of indescribable cruelty were told.

A Jewish violinist from the Opera had been made to scrub the streets. In the pail of water that he used an acid had been poured which took the flesh from his fingers.

A Jewish director of the Opera was taken from his box and beaten to a pulp. Someone found him by the roadside and he was removed to hospital. When he was released, his face marked for life, his body broken by

Cause and Effect

the blows of his assassins he went home and took poison.

An old Jew who had tried to protect his daughter from outrage had been beaten to death.

Believing such things could not be I went to see Dr. Neubacher, the Nazi Lord Mayor of Vienna, who had just been released from prison.

He received me with the utmost courtesy and his face was an honest one.

"Are these stories true?" I asked.

"They are true," he answered. "Remember though that in a revolution it is always the scum which rises first to the surface."

I walked from his office.

On the way back to my hotel I entered the cathedral. A little group of men, women and children were kneeling, and a cardinal was blessing them. His face was finely moulded. It had at once a gentleness and yet an imperiousness as though he were, indeed, a prince of the Church.

When the little service was over, he walked across the road with swift steps, as if his soul were in revolt against what was happening in his Austria. Quietly, and without speaking, his young priests followed him.

A few months later the mob stormed that very house. They were looking for the cardinal who had dared to raise his voice against the Nazi régime. They did not find him, but they threw a priest from the window, and broke both his legs. They burned and mutilated and violated the sacred things that were in the room, and tore the pictures from the wall. The Lord Mayor had said that it was the scum which always rose first to the surface in a revolution. With Nazism that scum never subsided.

When Austria went, the flank was turned for Czechoslovakia.

Can we at least say that the Czechoslovak State, that valuable and tragic experiment in democracy, was free from any responsibility for this war?

One had only to travel for a day in Czechoslovakia to realize how hopelessly it had been put together. Never was a structure built with such a foundation of disintegration. A genius might have created out of it another Switzerland. That genius did not arise. Masaryk was a great man but he was also a great patriot—and he was a Czech.

Dr. Benes was brave, shrewd and capable—but he was a Czech, and the memories of his people's wrongs were rooted deep in history.

The Sudeten Germans might have been won to the cause of the Republic. They had never really been part of the Reich. Their towns and their factories and their homes were German and yet not of Germany. The difference is a subtle one—but it was there.

Benes and Masaryk, great men as they were, allowed the hour to pass. Had they offered in 1936 or even in 1937 the terms they put forward in 1938, even Hitler might not have been able to have invented the persecution of the Sudeten minority, and what a mistake to resist the restoration of the Austrian monarchy!

Is Poland blameless?

To-day that ill-fated country is broken on the wheel of Russo-German domination. At the time of Munich Poland played a perilous role. Her rulers were not big enough to see that Czechoslovakia was an outpost of defence for themselves. All they could think of was the territory which the Czechs had stolen from them when Poland was at death grips with Russia in 1921. It was assumed that Poland would almost certainly be on Germany's side in the September crisis of 1938. That helped to inflame Hitler's mind and strengthen his purpose.

Is any country wholly blameless for this war?

Undoubtedly. There is Iceland.

Who then is chiefly responsible? There can be only one answer—Germany.

And who bears the second responsibility? To answer that question we must turn to the chapter on The Great Neutral.

CHAPTER III

The Two Germanys

IN THE SUMMER OF 1928 I PAID A VISIT TO Germany. The Allied armies of occupation still held the Rhineland. One saw the foreign soldiers about the streets there. The French were aloof, dignified, restrained, keeping apart from the people and kept apart by them. Only white troops remained. No longer did you glimpse the cloak of a Moorish Spahi or the squat Senegalese's scarlet cap. The Africans had gone, but they had left bitter memories behind them. Since the days of the Roman Empire the Rhineland had never been garrisoned by black soldiers. Worse than a crime, it was a blunder.

Street names were altered. French authority made its pleasure known by posting curt commands. The atmosphere was not cordial. I went on to the British area. There everything was free and easy. The Rhineland cities were recovering their spirits. The British Tommy was the lad of the village and sat sharing his mug of beer with the Rhine maidens.

On into Bavaria we journeyed through dark forests of fir trees and great silver lakes, past red-roofed villages and fields bright with harebells which the young deer went scampering over.

There was certainly distress in the great cities. There were week-end clashes between demonstrators with different opinions. But the Germany the traveller saw was certainly not an unhappy country. There was

The Two Germanys

an intensity of relief, an unaffected joyousness in the new Republic where young men and women felt not only lucky but also glad to be alive. Roving bands of young people swung bareheaded and bronzed between the trees where slashes of paint in different colours picked out the trail upon the tree trunks. They sang as they went the songs of their grandfathers to the notes of their guitars.

In the frank companionship of the sexes they unaffectedly enjoyed those summer days. To understand the Germany that Hitler created you had to see something of the Germany that Hitler destroyed. A splendid mania for the great out-of-doors had swept over the face of the land. Everywhere there sprang up stadia, sports grounds and swimming-pools, built, I have no doubt, with foreign loans. Every week-end the young people went camping and climbing. The first youth hostels were springing up on the remote hillsides, and the new generation of students dropped their duelling and took to football instead.

Two years later. 1930. This time a trip to Berlin. They were trying to make the stiff Prussian capital a focus of European gaiety.

It did not come off. The self-conscious and artificial effort to set it up evaporated in a gross and garish night-life that made the Friedrichstrasse noisy and unpleasant for 24 hours out of 24. But behind this tawdry face of things Berlin was still its stiff, unsophisticated provincial self. There were plenty of concert halls where your true Berliner went for his enjoyment. There were still two things that Hitler has since killed, decent unsubtle laughter and sincere applause.

Men, Martyrs and Mountebanks

When I went there again it was in 1934. The Nazis had been in power for just eighteen months. Their first purge was only a week old. Yet the change was unbelievable. One came to a city that was full of fear. Death hung in the air. There was a nightmare sense of horror that followed you everywhere you went. Business men actually walked the streets all night because they were afraid to go home. They thought the Brownshirts might be waiting there for them, although they did not know why.

All night you heard the clip-clop of heavy marching feet. Every morning your paper contained pathetic advertisements from wives, many of them living in the city's most wealthy suburbs, who asked for news, any news, about husbands not heard of for many days who went out at such a time and had not come home.

On the letter-heads of business firms the name of a certain partner would be blotted out in ink. Even at the Hotel Adlon the process eliminated a director or two at the top of the menu card. A friend advised me to buy the latest Nazi Who's Who. So I sent out for it.

It seems the pages were still in the printing press when the purge took place. The Nazi authorities first held up publication, then ordered certain omissions and finally commanded the work to appear. When the thing came out they had not bothered even to reset the type. There were great white gaps in the letterpress and blank slabs where photographs should have been. The entries had been listed alphabetically, but the space devoted to each had been regulated by the subject's importance to the Movement. So there were large blanks, medium blanks,

The Two Germanys

and small blanks. Instead of the entry for Von Schleicher was an empty half-column. Humbler victims of the firing squad had only an inch of white space for their epitaphs.

They brought the book out like that, and they sold it like that; truly a devilish thing. It could only have happened in Germany.

The city was full of uniforms. Those who still lacked the brown, black, grey or green outfits to which they were entitled, paraded in the army boots, leather belts and peaked caps that forecast the splendour to come.

The opera house that night was crowded with officers in uniform. Some of them were weedy little fellows, many had spectacles tilted over their noses. But they all trailed their swords around, with their obedient wives, who, innocent of make-up, dutifully trotted beside their lords and masters. The procession in the foyer kept, of course, to the strictly one-way traffic line which the Berlin opera audience always observes between the acts.

The opera was *Tosca*. The warmth and the passion of Puccini were never intended to carry the burden of the German language. Italian melody and German gutturals constituted an axis that also did not work.

After the second act we left by the Nord Express for Paris. Edgar Granville, the Parliamentary private secretary to Sir John Simon, then Foreign Minister, was with me. We talked together of this new Germany and we could do nothing but despair.

Next morning, about 70 miles short of Paris, our train came to a sudden standstill. Disturbed by the murmur of anxious voices around us, we went out to see what was wrong. The back axle of our engine had broken. One gigantic wheel was a full foot off the track, and its companion was leaning inwards. All night we had been racing across bridges and through cities with that axle working nearer and nearer to breaking-point. "That's Europe!" said Edgar Granville. Then and there we determined that he should take back this message to Sir John Simon: "Ask no questions. Join up with France and march to-morrow." Then we went into the *speiswagen* and had an *aperitif*.

What had happened to work the sinister transformation? I cannot easily forget the warm-hearted welcome the Bavarians and the Rhinelanders gave us who had been their enemies. These people are charming, their hospitality is unaffected. It may be rather gross sometimes, but it is generous and utterly sincere. But going East you meet a different strain. Always in Berlin you notice the yellowing skin, the narrow Mongol eyes, the square brutish head which betrays the Slav in every Prussian.

For your Prussian is essentially of the East. That is why he is always looking instinctively Eastwards. Perhaps, too, that is why he hates the Jew. Those two have a common origin somewhere in the Orient, where the robber is eternally at war with the merchant who cheats him in the market-place.

Side by side these two Germanys have gone on. Germany has the face of a Doktor Jekyll which it turns to its visitors, and the face of Herr Hyde which is hidden in the shadow. How did the Weimar Republic deal with this grim dual personality? Stresemann had great qualities. Considerable foresight was among them. He pleaded earnestly with the enemy for some mitigation in his people's lot. Just one big concession, he said, would make it possible for the Republic to live. Just one—or perhaps two.

But France was full of fear. At what stage would she have conceded enough to enable that Hyde face of Prussianism to show itself openly again? What moment would this monster select to clamp upon the expanding soul of young Germany the Prussian mould that is welded of blood and iron?

That was the quandary with which France and Britain were faced in the vital post-war years. Characteristically Dr. Bruening saw it, and characteristically Dr. Bruening understood. Characteristically, too, Dr. Bruening fumbled. He was a man with a fine intellect and a charming personality. Well read, cultured in his approach, quietly reasonable in discussion, he was a man with whom England would have talked and with whom in time England would have agreed. But all that time the Hitler menace was growing up in Germany and Dr. Bruening was the worst man to handle it.

With slow deliberation he applied the methods and measures of nineteenth century liberalism to the age-old savagery of the Nazis. He argued with atavistic instincts; he tried to defeat a monster by debate. To the very end he hated strong methods. He always distrusted strong men, even if they were on his side.

The essence of totalitarian tactics is this: they are dynamic. But the word 'dynamic' did not happen to be in Dr. Bruening's vocabulary.

He preferred to trust two things—the German's attachment to freedom which did not exist, and the

German's belief in Democracy which he had to create. To build Democracy in France has taken a century. In Britain it has taken three. Dr. Bruening could hardly set it up in Germany in a day. Besides, all history was against him.

Right down to 1914 Germany preserved her separate States. For centuries she was divided into a multitude of little units, almost all authoritarian. The local King, Grand Duke, Elector or Prince Bishop was always near enough to overshadow and to direct the life of the citizen.

So the German developed an instinct for obeying orders and a constitutional inability to think out anything for himself. Every point had to be explained to his understanding. In the short life of the post-war Weimar Republic there was generally a special party to explain every point. Over twenty political parties contended for the votes of the poor puzzled elector, and as German thoroughness had worked out the most perfect machine ever devised to give each party the precise weight in the National Assembly to which its strength entitled it, there was always a stalemate in the Government. Besides, no German can grasp more than one idea at a time. Having duly accepted the thesis advanced by one of the twenty parties, his mind was closed completely to the point of view of the other nineteen. He held that anybody who thought otherwise than himself was either a fool or a traitor, probably both. Sir Nevile Henderson has said: "Two of the less attractive characteristics of the German are his inability to see any side of a question but his own, and his inability to understand the machinery of moderation."

The Two Germanys

The average Englishman, whose ignorance of his friends' politics is only equalled by his indifference to them, cannot easily understand the extent to which political loyalties cut across German life between 1919 and 1933. Among those bands of loyal friends who roamed through the fair fields of Thuringia, the Harz and the Bavarian highlands (until Hitler made them march over them) there was, as I have said, little consciousness of sex. There was also little consciousness of either age or class. But there was a very strong consciousness of party. You might find men and women, schoolboys and greyheads, miners and counts climbing and canoeing together. But you could not find Conservatives and Socialists.

Hitler throve on those distinctions, although he condemned them. They persisted among the supporters of the Weimar Republic to the end—and after.

At no time did a majority of the German people freely give their confidence to the Nazis. But at no time did that majority combine to oppose them. The twenty parties squabbled on till they were slaughtered together. Thus Hitler was able to destroy his opponents piecemeal by striking in turn at the Communists, the Socialists, the Liberals, the Conservatives, the Protestants and the Catholics with all the grim armoury of persecution and proscription against which no section ever protested until it was directed against itself.

. . . . . .

Could Britain have saved the Weimar Republic?

I imagine that historians will go on to the end of time arguing whether the present War would or would not have been avoided if we had treated the German Republic more generously. Three years after Hitler came into power, Dr. Bruening told me that if he had been given one-fifth of what Hitler took, peace in Europe would have been saved for a century.

Germany certainly had deep grievances in the years between the Peace of Versailles and the coming of Hitler, although she added to their number by inventing twice as many that did not exist.

It was an error of the French to send black regiments into the Rhineland. It was petty to hedge Germany's entry into the League of Nations in 1926 with so many restrictions that the gesture lost its value. A friend of mine, an Englishman, was in a Hamburg café when the news came out that Germany had been voted into the League.

The scene was extraordinary. Special leaflets issued from the Press were passed eagerly from hand to hand over the tables. 'Germany in the League.' People jumped up on their chairs to drink toasts. My friend had his arm nearly twisted from its socket by hearty handshakes and he could have been treated to enough beer to fill the great tun at Heidelberg.

Then came all the petty chicane. To offset Germany's seat on the League Council an extra place was created for Brazil, which was supposed to be an ally of France. I do not remember all that happened ultimately. Neither does anybody else. But the end of it all was that by the time Germany got her seat the whole effect of the great gesture was almost completely dissipated. Had my friend still been in Hamburg he could not have got one half-pint without paying for it.

The Two Germanys

It should have been the prelude to a new world order. They turned it into one more grievance of an age-long quarrel.

If German Youth turned to Hitler in the spring of 1933 you could not entirely blame them. They had seen defeat, civil war, inflation and disillusionment.

A story was told to a British visitor to Oberammergau in 1922 which typifies the hopelessness of their world during the inflation. Some village children were given minor parts in the Passion play. They were promised a certain amount of money, enough to buy some toys on which they had set their hearts, but they were only to be paid at the end of the season. Patiently they waited and duly they were paid. By then the value of the mark had slumped again. The money would not buy the toys. They could not understand what had happened.

No German could understand what had happened. He only knew that in that mad world of collapsing values there was no King, no Grand Duke, no War Lord in shining armour to look after him.

Of course, there was the Republican government. But the Republican government told him to have confidence in himself. And that is the one thing the German never has had. That is why he likes to go about in bands. He is uncomfortable by himself. There is only one place where he is even more uncomfortable. That is, in the company of a foreigner. I don't think it is a coincidence that the 'Inferiority Complex' was discovered in Germany.

It may be because his country is a newcomer among the nations. After all, his grandfather was still fighting for Hanover against Prussia or for Hesse against Hanover.

It may be that he feels that he is not quite inside the Community of Western Europe. He never shared Roman civilization with the rest of us. Or perhaps it is just the awkwardness of people who have become powerful too quickly. It was to reassure themselves that the Germans, before 1914, used to go about boasting of their victories, their iron strength, their great wealth and super-efficiency. And suddenly they had been defeated, their unity was reft by civil war. Their credit was worthless. To many young Germans of the 1920's there were only three ways out : World Revolution. Emigration. Suicide.

Then they began to hear of Hitler. A fantastic figure in a brown shirt and a scrub moustache was shrieking his way round the meeting halls of South Germany. Much of what he said was quite incomprehensible. Much of it they knew to be utterly untrue. The company he kept was notoriously bad, for he was surrounded by perverts, drug addicts, and criminals, even if they were diluted with bemused idealists and war heroes. Yet, there was no getting away from it, he explained away their troubles and he showed them the way out.

They were the finest people in the world. Quite right ! Then how had they come to lose the war? They had not lost it. They had been betrayed by the Jews. Their Unity was indeed made of iron. But the Marxists had misled their simple honest natures and driven them to civil war. Their credit was magnificent, only for the moment they had been betrayed by International Finance. Once diagnosed, the ill

The Two Germanys

was easy to cure. The German race being the finest in the world, it was only necessary to keep its bloodstream pure. As the Marxists were breaking up their Unity, the cure was to get rid of the Marxists. And since International Finance had ruined German credit, Germany must break away from the chains of International Finance. Which meant she must not pay her debts. The German people were not convinced at once. Some of them even saw the ridiculous side. "The root of all our ills is the Jews," cries the Nazi propagandist.

"That's right," said Hans, the last German left with a sense of humour. "The Jews and the people on tricycles."

"But why the people on tricycles?" the agitator asked.

"Well, if it comes to that, why the Jews?" said Hans.

There was a devilish ingenuity about the Nazi appeal. It satisfied three fundamentals in the German's nature. It met his craving for the lost leadership by providing one, a leader whom all Germans had to obey. It flattered his inferiority complex by telling him he belonged to a superior race. It pandered to his herd instinct, putting him into uniform and marching him around in "groups" and "standards" singing the Horst Wessel song in chorus. And it touched, too, that chord of savagery that runs through the race (you need not go beyond Grimm's Fairy Tales to discover it) by letting him loose on Jews, gypsies, Marxists and other inferior and misguided persons. And after having his country occupied by the French it was a relief to be able to beat up the Jews.

There was the other Germany, of course, the

Germany I saw in 1928, the Germany that gave us the great masters in music and literature and science, the Germany of Beethoven, Goethe, Ehrlich and Dr. Bruening. In its death agony that Germany went down pointing an accusing finger at France and ourselves. "You set us up and you suffered us to perish. You compounded with our executioners."

I have argued that you could not blame the German people for putting Hitler in. But can they be acquitted of responsibility in the crimes that he committed and that they allowed in the name of discipline? There is no point in going over all the atrocities of Hitler's five years in power. Some day he will account for those thousands of mangled corpses that disappeared from his concentration camps, his prisons, and his Brown Houses to which people were carried away without a trial. Some day a chronicler may catalogue the countless visits that were paid in those days to the homes of innocent men at dawn; the times a horrified householder, whose only crime was his faith in democracy or his possession of Jewish blood, looked out and saw the S.S. men in their black uniforms and heavy black helmets tumble out of a lorry in the street below. He knew then what was going to happen, that he would just vanish, leaving no trace till his ashes were delivered at the door. Nobody was going to ask any questions. What matters is that the German people collectively never once objected. They stood there with their arms lifted, shouting "Heil Hitler!" while their elected representatives were being stamped to death. They cheered when Pastor Niemoeller was acquitted, but they made no protest when he was thrown into a concentration camp.

The Two Germanys

They worshipped the leader who instigated his dupes to murder the head of Austria, a neighbour State. And they named streets and squares after the murderers.

Worst of all, they never ceased prostrating themselves before the Government that taught their children to deny their God and to denounce their parents. "I think," wrote a British Consul when he was reporting on the racial atrocities of November 1938, "that Hitler knows his Germans." Well, perhaps the French know them too. They, after all, are their neighbours and have had very good opportunities of getting acquainted with them.

Once an apostle of conciliation asked the late M. Clemenceau whether his hatred of the Germans was based on any knowledge whatever. "Have you ever been to Germany?" he was asked. "No, Monsieur," replied the Tiger, "I have never been to Germany. But twice in my lifetime the Germans have been to France."

And there was someone else who knew them. Heinrich Heine, till the Nazis discovered the natural inferiority of the Semite, was Germany's favourite poet. His songs were sung at every concert and gathering. The songs are still sung, only the Germans have ceased to acknowledge the authorship.

Heinrich Heine wrote this about Germany in 1834:

> One day our natural philosophers will be more terrible through being allied with certain elemental forces in our nature. They will call on the old German gods. They will conjure up our inherent lust for battle; a lust that yearns neither to

conquer nor to destroy but to fight for fighting's sake.

Christianity rendered a great service by restraining that German lust for war. Restrained, I say. It did not destroy it. One day you will see the Cross broken and all the savagery of our ancient warriors resurrected. The Cross is a very brittle emblem after all. One day it will be shattered. The old stone gods will rub the dust of 1,000 years out of their eyes and the hammer of Thor will shatter all our Gothic steeples. Be you 'ware in those days, neighbour peoples. You Frenchmen beware. I have been horrified to see that your ministers want to disarm you. Do not forget that high on Olympus where the gods eat Ambrosia and quaff Nectar, there dwells one goddess who, while all around her take their ease, is always in armour and wears a helmet and carries a spear. She is the goddess of wisdom.

Goethe was Germany's greatest writer. He, too, knew his fellow countrymen.

A few months ago a friend of mine was walking in the Harz mountains with his German host, who paused before a certain hill.

"You see that peak? Hitler is going to speak from there on Sunday."

My friend said politely that it was very interesting.

"Yes, isn't it? Now I'll tell you something more. That was the peak where, according to the legend, Mephistopheles the evil one appeared to Faust. That is where he offered him worldly success in return for his soul."

The Two Germanys

My friend, a little embarrassed, did not know how to answer.

"And you know whom Goethe meant to portray by Faust?"

My friend shook his head.

"We. We, the German people. We are Faust," said the other sadly.

Perhaps in the sardonic honesty of that man's mind, in the world-mindedness of Dr. Bruening, in the healthy companionship of the young men and women as they walked the lovely roads of Bavaria, we shall yet re-discover and re-create the other Germany.

CHAPTER IV

At the German Embassy

THERE CAN NEVER BE ANY DOUBT THAT Hitler was perfectly sincere when, from the very beginning of his public career, he stressed the importance of friendship with Great Britain.

There is no question but that he would have welcomed an Anglo-German alliance with the feeling that the two nations could control the world and ensure peace for fifty years.

When Sir John Simon went to Berlin in 1933, and had an interview with Hitler, even his legal calm was jolted when the Fuehrer made the cool proposal that Germany would assist Britain in running her Empire. Hitler was on his good behaviour on that occasion, and did not realize the crudity of what he was saying. The only empire that he could conceive was one that was held in submission by an all-powerful central State. Why should not German strength ally itself to Britain's strength, and make of the Colonies and Dominions, not mere outposts of peace, but outposts of power? There is no record of what Sir John Simon, as Foreign Secretary, said to the German Chancellor at that time—his thoughts, however, can be easily assessed.

Quite rightly Hitler regarded the German Embassy in London as a most important factor in developing this policy of friendship with Britain. Therefore he chose his men with the greatest possible care. His

At the German Embassy

first and best Ambassador was von Hoesch, whom he confirmed in his existing appointment.

This man was the very finest type of German. He was tall, immaculate, good-looking, and although of a recognized military type, he was in reality a citizen of the world. As Ambassador to Paris he had laboured sincerely to bring to an end the difference between his country and the French. When death struck him down in London, it was a bad day for civilization. He had moral courage, a quality which was dwindling fast under the Nazi régime. I talked with him a few days before his death, and felt what everyone did, the essential fineness of his spirit.

There was, however, as counsellor at the Embassy, a more colourful personality in Prince Otto von Bismarck, the grand-son of the great Chancellor.

Bismarck was young, serious and ambitious. He had the asset of having married one of the most beautiful women in Europe—Ann Mari Tengbom, of Sweden, whom he had met during his time at the Legation in Sweden. At the opera, in the drawing-rooms of Mayfair, and at Frinton-on-Sea, where they had a summer home, the Princess moved in an aura of exquisite beauty and abundant charm. Bismarck, being a German, lacked finesse, for all his efforts to acquire it. She always recovered any ground that he might have lost. With admirable regularity she continued to bear him children—no fewer than three being born in this country, and after each child she seemed, if anything, more radiant than before.

Because Hitler was not in a strong position when he first took power, Bismarck did his best to placate opinion in this country. On the whole he was a good servant to his master. He accepted such criticism of the administration as we might make, and gave his replies with a courtesy which only now and then broke down. It was not easy for Bismarck to be a pleader for the Austrian sign-painter who sat in the seat of his grandfather.

In 1936 he was recalled to Berlin to take charge of the British Department of the Foreign Office. We wished him well in good French champagne, and we covered the Princess with such compliments as might well have turned a less pretty head. A few months after his departure I met them at St. Moritz, where the usual motley, international assembly had gathered for winter sports. It was a different Bismarck.

No longer was there that subtle suggestion of deference. In fact, there was no deference at all.

"How is Germany getting on?" I asked.

"I think perhaps," he answered, "it is more important for me to ask how Britain is getting on. You seem to be having a certain amount of trouble."

There was nothing memorable in the dialogue. The significance lay entirely in the manner. When, next day, von Bismarck dislocated his shoulder, I received the news with a calm which surprised even myself.

The man who followed von Hoesch was, of course, von Ribbentrop.

We did not know a great deal about him, save for his romantic escape from Canada in the first world war, and that he was a wine merchant who had married into an aristocratic vineyard in Germany.

Young Fritz Randolph, Press attaché at the German Embassy, went to meet him at the boat.

At the German Embassy

"I come here with only one purpose," said Ribbentrop to his colleague, "I come as the realization of a dream to bring about the friendship of Germany with England."

That statement was not made for British ears, but to a member of his own staff. Yet when he left this country after a comparatively short Ambassadorship he was as inveterate an enemy of ours as ever could breathe. I don't suppose the faults were entirely on his side. He lacked diplomatic training, and possessed few of the niceties which mark the conduct of the *corps diplomatique*. He lacked an outer covering to his skin. Every insult made him bleed, every imagined slight pricked him, every difference of opinion infuriated him. When he presented his credentials to His Majesty the King he gave the Nazi salute. It does not seem a particularly grievous offence, looking back on it, but it started the rumours that a tactless fellow was in our midst. Similar stories multiplied themselves. His pale face and colourless eyes bespoke a constrained resentment. He complained in private that when he called at the Foreign Office to see Anthony Eden, the young clerks would send up a message to tell the Secretary of State that the wine merchant had arrived. Whether it is true or not does not matter greatly. He believed that it was. Another story went the rounds that caused him immense indignation. It was to the effect that a visitor had called upon the French Ambassador in London, and had noticed a painting of Talleyrand.

"I suppose," he said, "that Talleyrand was the most successful Ambassador that France ever had in London?"

Men, Martyrs and Mountebanks

"No," said the Ambassador, "Ribbentrop."

During Ribbentrop's régime in London the German Embassy grew more grim with each succeeding month. There was never any gaiety there, but always a sense of strain which struck one the moment the door was opened. I lunched with Ribbentrop at the House of Commons together with a number of my fellow M.P.s just before he left for home.

We had small cause to love him, for while he was Ambassador to our country he had fashioned the anti-Comintern Pact, and had gone to Berlin to sign it with Japan.

It was typical of the utter tactlessness which possessed him at all times that he should have made this journey and completed this project while holding the position which he did. However, when our lunch came to an end, Ribbentrop made a short speech.

"It is the duty," he said, "of engineers to build roads to link countries together. It is the duty of diplomats to build bridges of peace which link the nations of the world in the common effort for civilization."

His English was perfect, and in his unsmiling eyes there seemed a real sincerity. Blunderer, braggart, and schemer as he was, it might have been better if we had not shown so clearly that we recognized him for what he was—an Iago without Iago's brains.

No one could have been more different than his successor, Dr. von Dircksen.

I called to see him at the Embassy three or four days after his arrival, when the worthy Doctor was looking at everything with the innocent, startled eyes of a kitten which finds itself in unaccustomed

At the German Embassy

surroundings. The Embassy seemed less grim than it had been before, but still a bare and ugly place. Downstairs there was a huge painting of Hitler with a moustache which pointed upwards until it almost rivalled that of the ex-Kaiser. Upstairs in the Ambassador's room there was another painting of Herr Hitler, where the moustache had slumped to its normal shape.

Dr. von Dircksen was a great collector of china. He was a stout, large man, with a slightly apologetic manner, and a complete lack of military bearing. He could not have frightened even the representative of a small nation. He liked pictures and music, but especially he liked collecting old and rare things. Nothing could have been more friendly than his reception of myself, and although we were to meet many times after that, often in difficult circumstances, he never failed to express the friendliest sentiments. He gave me the impression at all times of being completely isolated from Berlin, and I think that impression may have been a true one. Von Hoesch and von Ribbentrop had been definite and powerful figures. Dr. von Dircksen, one felt, had come to fill the gap and little more. That he was a man of peace no one could doubt. That he was utterly unable to do anything to preserve peace is equally beyond question. With the coming of Dr. von Dircksen, however, there also arrived a man of considerable character and ability.

I refer to Dr. Kordt, the new First Secretary to the German Embassy. It was Dr. Kordt who subsequently waved "good-bye" at the aerodrome to Mr. Chamberlain as he took off for Munich. It was the same

Dr. Kordt on the morning of September 3rd, 1939, who received from Mr. Chamberlain the news of our ultimatum—and war.

Shortly after his arrival I was asked to lunch with him privately at the home of Count von Pückler, the young German journalist who later wrote that surprisingly frank book, *How Strong is England?*

The contrast between Pückler and Kordt was a striking one. Kordt was a serious schoolmaster type of man lacking in elegance, but with an efficient brain. Pückler had all the ease and humour of the aristocratic dilettante. He had a style of humour which was peculiar to himself. His voice would get more and more gloomy as his remarks grew more and more frivolous. On the other hand, beneath the badinage, there was an understanding of the world which far outstripped that of any of the other Germans who were stationed in London during those "post-war pre-war" days.

Although there were only three of us at lunch, Dr. Kordt was showing every sign of being ultra-cautious. He confined himself to platitudes and compliments, but would not venture into the quagmire of controversy. Feeling the uselessness of this conversation, I finally tried to break it down by saying to him: "If your country and mine should go to war again, then the curse of history will be upon us."

To my surprise he suddenly stood up, and with upraised, trembling hands, cried: "Every word of what you say is true. The curse of history and the curse of God would be upon our peoples."

It was such a startling change in him that I could hardly believe my eyes. It was as if the self-imposed

At the German Embassy

restraint of years had broken down in that strange and unexpected moment.

"I must say one more thing," I went on. "If this war does come, it will be Germany's fault and we shall fight with twice the strength and twice the purpose of 1914."

Von Pückler lit a cigarette. "You will need to," he said coolly.

But of all the men at the Embassy, the ablest was undoubtedly the good-looking young Dr. Fitz Randolph.

He was understandably popular in London, although rumour had it that he was in fact a German spy. Such accusations did not influence me greatly, since diplomats the world over must see what they see and report in due course. He may have gone beyond that, but it does not necessarily concern us here.

As his name indicates, he came of a family with English associations. It was, in fact, four hundred years ago that an English Fitz Randolph settled in what is now called the Reich.

The Doctor was singularly well equipped to take a broader view of affairs than his colleagues. His mother was an American and, I think, still lives in the United States. He himself was born there but left at the age of five and went to Paris, where he stayed until he was thirteen. Then he moved to Berlin and pursued his education until, at the age of twenty, he returned to America and attended college there. Thus he had the blessing of languages and the ripeness of wide experience.

When the Germans marched into Prague in the spring of 1939 the anger which swept Britain was intense and bitter. Never before or since has our hatred of Hitler reached such a pitch. In everything else which the German dictator had done he had been able to make some plausible excuse by stretching the truth a yard or so.

At Prague he deliberately struck the Democracies across the face. Munich was over. No longer did the superman need to consider the Governments of France and Britain. The fury of the British Press almost burned the pages as they were printed. For no particular reason I thought of Fitz Randolph. I could well imagine that the German Embassy had suddenly become an isolated plague spot. I called him on the telephone and he answered with an unusual gruffness. In reply to an invitation to lunch with me, he said curtly that he was otherwise engaged. I told him he was lying.

"You had better come and have lunch with me," I said, "for no one else will give it you to-day."

"Very well," he snapped. "When and where?"

We met at the Carlton Club annexe at half-past one. It was after four o'clock when he said 'goodbye.' For nearly three hours we talked as man to man without reticence and without duplicity. His fine features were clouded with a sadness which gave him an undoubted dignity. He had come in 1933 to London as one of the first appointees of Hitler. For nearly eight years he had followed the tortuous path of Anglo-German relations and now in London he was surrounded by a sea of hate which chilled and startled and discouraged him.

"What has happened to England?" he asked.

At the German Embassy

"Last September at Munich she was like this. . . ." He made a wobbling gesture with his hand indicative of weakness. "Now," he went on, "she is of one mind. She is ready for war. I don't need to be told that, I know it. Never have I felt this country so united and determined as at this moment."

"We owe that to your man, Hitler," I said. "Will you tell him so, with our thanks?"

"I do not see Hitler," he said. "It is true that I make my journey to Germany once a month or so but the Fuehrer only sees the men at the very top."

"But in Heaven's name," I asked, "wouldn't even the Fuehrer send for you, who have been here all through his régime, to ask your advice?"

For a few minutes we discussed the German leader. He with that curious sense of reverence and myself with a courtesy which ill bespoke my thoughts.

"The trouble is," he said, "that there is a psychological no-man's-land between the Germans and the British. We go so far in understanding one another—but only so far. Then we come to the no-man's-land which neither side can cross. You have had individual freedom for hundreds of years and value it above everything. We have not had it. We think of making our place in the world by strength and sacrifice and death on the battlefield. You say: 'Let's talk about it. Let's talk about everything. There is nothing so serious that it cannot be talked about.' We say: 'There is nothing so small that it cannot be dealt with by action.' You despise uniforms, we take pride in them. To you a uniform is an abrogation of your rights as a citizen. To us it is a boast of our citizenship.

"All the trouble between us is psychological. You cannot understand us and we cannot understand you. It is tragic, deplorable."

I suggested that two people could have friendship without complete understanding and that in Britain there had always been a genuine liking for Germany until Hitler began to make that liking impossible.

Fitz Randolph smiled for the first time. "Yes," he said, "I believe you like us in some ways, but I think you like us better when we are weak than when we are strong."

He was very pleased with that remark and repeated it to enjoy its flavour a second time. I was going to answer that perhaps Germany was more lovable when she was less strong, but I left it unsaid. After all, a German in London at that time was too easy a target. When we reached Pall Mall he put out his hand. "There is one thing," he said, "which we cannot do anything against—your propaganda. It is so magnificent, so incredibly good. It is what we fear most."

With some surprise I explained that much to my regret we had no Ministry of Propaganda nor any means of consultation between the newspapers.

"No, no, no," he said ; "I know that. It is just this. . . . Every British subject is a born propagandist. He does not have to be taught to do it. He does it. You yourself will go this summer to the United States or Canada for your holiday. Wherever you are you will seize every opportunity to do propaganda for England. Will anybody tell you to do it ? Will anybody thank you when you have done it ?

At the German Embassy

Will you get paid for it? If this war comes, your propaganda will have the world against us before we start."

With an unconscious irony he brought his heels together and bowed. "I must go back to the Embassy," he said. "I will never forget your kindness."

"If you become a prisoner of war," I said, "let me know and I shall send you British newspapers to read."

For the second time he smiled. "I have already sent instructions," he said, "that if London is bombed your house is not to be hit."

The fury over the march into Prague receded but did not disappear. As summer approached we found ourselves once more believing that the war might be avoided. Von Dircksen told me that the feeling in Germany was much better and that Danzig would be settled without any trouble.

Later, in July, came word that Fitz Randolph had been recalled. Rumour had it that he was in disgrace, that he had been talking too freely. Counter-rumours were that he had done so well that he was being promoted. At any rate, Baron von Hahn, whose duty it was to rise at five every morning, read the British papers and telephone the contents to Berlin at 8 o'clock, decided to give a farewell luncheon at his flat for the returning exile. The luncheon consisted of von Hahn and his wife, four or five members of the German Embassy, Bernard Rickatson-Hatt—the Editor of Reuters—Fitz Randolph, my wife and myself.

Towards the end of the luncheon the Germans were in good spirits. After all, it was a somewhat unusual experience to find themselves in a majority—and

Men, Martyrs and Mountebanks

Germany's wines had done their duty. At last the host turned to me and said: "Now that our friend, Fitz Randolph, is leaving us, won't you tell him for his education why you dislike the Nazis so much. We think we are pretty good fellows and we cannot understand why you don't think so, too."

A jovial thumping of the table supported the host's demand for a reply.

"It is difficult to put it into words," I said, "but since you have asked me to do so, I will try. We are all at this table men and women of the world. Anyone of you would be willing to tell an amusing story about Chamberlain or the Archbishop of Canterbury or even to make fun about Westminster Abbey. We are a Democracy and we reserve the right to treat our masters as our equals. But look at you Germans here. You are all cynics, you are all realists, and none of you are humbugs, yet which of you at this table is prepared to say that Adolf Hitler is less than God?"

There was a sudden and almost ludicrous silence. No one spoke and every face was deadly serious. Fitz Randolph made the first attempt to end the silence.

"Of course," he said, "we all know, Baxter, that you are a *farceur*. You make good jokes."

I assured him that on this occasion I was not making a joke of any kind.

"After all, I am not asking very much," I said; "merely that one of you should admit that, great as Hitler is, majestic and sublime as he is, he is still less than God."

This time the silence remained unbroken. Then the hostess rose. The luncheon was over.

At the German Embassy

Rickatson-Hatt and I drove down to Fleet Street together. We both had the same feeling—that we had seen something ironic yet tragic. A race of men who had surrendered their very manhood in their fear of a system which had raised a second-rate Austrian sign-painter to the level of the Supreme Being.

Chapter V

An Empire Answers

FROM THE VERY OUTSET THE NAZI WAR scheme confidently based itself on the failure of the British Empire to make a united effort.

It was true that the vast Union of Peoples that went under the name of the British Empire comprised, with its Associates, Protectorates and Mandates, one out of every four people living on the earth, that its territories were to be found on every continent, that there was no sea that did not wash its shores.

But the Nazis could discover few outward signs that this great colossus of nations would hold together against a formidable shock. With the Teutonic gift for detail, they made out for themselves an unanswerable case.

Among five hundred million people there were rather less than a hundred thousand British soldiers to keep the peace.

In all that mixture of races, creeds, and colours, among which no strain, no belief, and no hue was unrepresented, there were fewer than fourteen million whites. And to these fourteen million every nation in Europe contributed its quota, not excluding those with whom Great Britain was at war. Within the framework of Empire large populations of French, Spaniards, Dutch, Greeks, Italians, Germans and Russians lived in separate communities governed by their own laws and maintaining their several customs.

An Empire Answers

The links that bound these various units to their centre were of varying degrees of strength, but for the most part they amounted to little beyond sentiment and tradition.

The Statute of Westminster had made independent nations out of the four great self-governing Dominions—Canada, South Africa, Australia and New Zealand. They were attached to Great Britain by no stronger tie than a common monarchy and a right of appeal to the same Supreme Court—the Judicial Committee of the Privy Council.

Their populations were predominantly white, but by no means overwhelmingly British. In Canada the British were a bare majority, in South Africa they were not a majority at all.

The British Empire, so thought the Nazi experts, was no longer the Empire of twenty-five years ago.

A German once scoffed at the British Empire as being held together by moonbeams. He might have reflected that a moonbeam is difficult to cut.

Yet the Nazis believed that the facts of contemporary history bore out their theory that the Union would not bear the strain of a second world war. In 1914 it was true that many Empire peoples had actually marched shoulder to shoulder till victory was won, although even then the Germans had called it a colossus standing like Nebuchadnezzar's image, on feet of clay. But they comforted themselves that the unity had not been so wholehearted as the British made out.

To bring South Africa in on Britain's side in 1914 had required a Civil War, in which 10,000 Boers, who had fought Britain fourteen years before, took up arms under two heroes of their former struggle for independence—Generals Byers and De Wet. It was true that 20,000 other Boers—under two greater heroes with equal experience in fighting against British troops—Generals Botha and Smuts—moved speedily and successfully against the rebels under the Union Jack.

But the incident was there to point out, and it was one that all good Nazis were taught to remember.

In 1914, too, the French population of Canada, numbering nearly a third of the whole, had been for the most part opposed to the war at the beginning, and apathetic about it at its close. There were some internal blunders that helped to cause this, but basically the fact remains.

In India there had been serious riots, in Ireland a full-dress rebellion. And Hitler reflected that conditions seemed to have deteriorated in the twenty years that had passed since then. Ireland had become independent and was under the Presidency of Eamon de Valera, whom the British had condemned to death in 1916. All the Dominions, with their own representatives on the League of Nations and, in many cases, their Ministers in foreign capitals, had so increased in population and economic strength as to be able to stand as the separate nations which, in effect, they were.

At Geneva they were free to vote against the mother country—and did so more than once.

The wave of nationalism that passed over the world in the 'twenties and 'thirties had not spared the British Empire. In South Africa both the Union Jack and *God Save the King* had been replaced by home-made substitutes.

An Empire Answers

General Hertzog, the Prime Minister, had advocated secession when in opposition, and neutrality when in office.

India had been torn by a campaign of civil disobedience directed by the Congress Party under the remarkable leadership of Mahatma Gandhi and the even more astute and determined Pandit Nehru. There was an agitation in Cyprus for return to Greece. Malta was troubled with Pan-Italian intrigues stimulated from Italy.

In South-West Africa, Hitler counted on his Germans, who comprised a third of the white population of 30,000. Tanganyika Territory contained 6,000 Germans to 9,000 British settlers. In both provinces Nazi propaganda, so fruitfully employed in Austria and Sudetenland, was used. Germany confidently counted on an armed rising.

The economic distress of the West Indies, where it is impossible to acquit the British Government of negligence, had resulted in an all-round lowering of British prestige within the Empire. On the spot, there were grim strikes led by the persuasive and powerful agitator, Bustamente.

Britain's enemies counted, too, on the condition of Palestine.

This country, half the size of Wales, required 50,000 British troops to keep order among a million people.

Two-thirds of the population were Arabs incensed at a flow of Jewish immigration that seemed to threaten them with minority status in their own country. The remainder was Jewish, embittered and disillusioned to see the prospects of a national home fading at the very moment when their persecuted co-racials most needed a refuge. For two years the rival races were only kept from each other's throats by a British garrison that suffered heavy casualties at the task. It was not a year since a rebel Jerusalem had been stormed by the Coldstream Guards. From his exile in Syria the Grand Mufti, Hajamine el Husseini, was conducting a fierce campaign against Britain.

Nazi Germany, allowing for her limited knowledge, had every logical reason to set high hopes on the Empire breaking up.

But the Germans have never been able to understand the voluntary basis of the British Empire. They believed that the whole of it was patrolled day and night by English sentries. Once an English guest in a family of highly intelligent Frankfurt Jews pointed out that Britain, like Germany, had its unemployment problem.

"But why don't you give them jobs as police in your colonies," asked his hosts.

Germans had noted with satisfaction the rise of South African Nationalism. They had watched Canada drawing economically close to the U.S.A. Their government, too, paid attention to an incident in 1937 when President Roosevelt did a most unusual and unexpected thing.

At the opening of a bridge on the Dominion border he publicly stood forth and, before an amazed world, took it upon himself to pledge the whole strength of the United States to the defence of Canada's integrity.

It seemed to loosen Canada from the Empire fabric, to draw her farther away from the Imperial orbit.

The loyalty of Australia and New Zealand was, indeed, never in doubt. Yet it did not seem over

An Empire Answers

optimistic for a patriotic German, brought up on Nazi propaganda, to hope that both countries would, in the event of war, be immobilized by a common fear of Japan.

Besides, the Nazi drew certain deductions from his own experience.

In a thousand centuries of its history their Holy Roman Empire was never once spiritually united in any war. Nor was the third Reich a great improvement on the first, save in the greater efficiency of its police methods. It required a quarter of a million Storm Troopers to hold down the Czechs—a hundred thousand more were permanently stationed in Austria.

In comparing their new conquests with the four-century-old British Empire, the Nazis were obviously much guided by wish-fulfilment. But it was by no means only Germans who looked to a slow disintegration, if not precisely to a violent snapping, of all Imperial connections.

There were Englishmen as well who doubted if the miracle of 1914 would be repeated. Who could imagine that in 1939 it would actually be enhanced?

Within ten days of the declaration of war every fragment of that Empire to its remotest islands, with one single exception, was busy raising men and money to fight for Britain.

The exception was Southern Ireland, a story that remains the same the more it alters.

Ireland would have no part in the common effort. Yet Irishmen in thousands came forward to fight for Britain.

At any rate, the enemy had set his highest hopes not

on Ireland, but on Palestine, and it was precisely from Palestine that he was to get his first disagreeable forecast of the truth.

Before the war was actually declared strange things had already been happening in Jerusalem. The Arab Defence Party, led by Raghid Bey Nashashibi claimed to represent a majority of the Arab population, and was possibly entitled to speak for about half of it. Although they had opposed the extremist methods advocated by the Grand Mufti, they had in the past been highly critical of British policy. Yet it did not even need a formal declaration of war to swing Nashashibi's followers into a wholehearted active support of Great Britain.

The Bey himself called on the High Commissioner, Sir Howard Macmichael, with a delegation of notables to place their properties and their lives unreservedly at his disposal.

No community had been more fierce in their opposition to the Jewish immigration than the Arab population of Jaffa, who had watched the prosperity of their ancient port being steadily overshadowed by the mushroom expansion of the adjoining suburb of Tel Aviv. Yet as soon as war was formally declared the chairman of the Jaffa Municipal Commission, Abdul Naouf Effendi Bitar, opened a register of volunteers, and began to enrol A.R.P. wardens.

By the second week of September the entire Arab community, whether moderate or extremist, was being swept by a wave of pro-British enthusiasm that was as unaccountable as it was unexpected.

"The war," wrote one of the Arab newspapers, *Falestin*, "has put all our relations with Great Britain

An Empire Answers

on a new basis. The Arab peoples have made up their minds to be on the side of democracy. No Arab who has the interest of his country at heart is willing to be an enemy of Britain."

"The Arabs of Palestine," wrote the other Arab newspaper, *Aldefaa*, "will not deviate from the path taken by their brethren. They have publicly expressed their loyalty and stressed their traditional friendship with the British nation."

Meanwhile, Arab volunteers were pouring in to offer their services from Dan even unto Beersheba. The Emir of Transjordania drove up to Government House through crowds of his cheering people to pledge his loyalty. Two thousand cultivators at Arraba spontaneously gathered to pledge every possible assistance to Britain. Even the Bedouins of the southern desert offered their "loyal co-operation" through their Sheikh. Most remarkable of all was the action of Hajamine el Husseini, the rebel Mufti, now a fugitive in Syria, whence he proclaimed . . . "Our Palestine Arabs will do nothing which could impede France or reflect on her interests."

The Palestine Jews formed in themselves a microcosm of contemporary Europe. There was every type among them. From the orthodox tillers of the soil whose forefathers had dwelt on the land in the days of Solomon, to the newest and slickest flivver-driving immigrant from New York's East Side, from the pedlar out of Eastern Europe's ghettoes, ragged, illiterate and bemused, to the uprooted professor of Vienna University, they covered the whole of human kind in all its infinite diversity.

To the great majority it would seem the British

Empire could have had very little meaning. Yet within a fortnight 92 per cent had volunteered their services for the defence of Palestine, while 50,000 expressed themselves ready to fight for the British Empire wherever they might be needed.

Meanwhile, the neighbouring Arab kingdoms were ranging themselves successively with the Allied cause. Egypt had, since the Caliphate was abruptly terminated in 1918 by Mustapha Kemal, inherited much of the moral leadership in Islam previously enjoyed by the Sultans of Turkey. Egypt, faithful to her alliance, broke off all relations with Germany. Even the Nationalist and previously anti-British Waafd opposition made common cause with King Farouk's royal government, in which it agreed to share till the struggle ended. Her example was quickly followed by Transjordania, Irak, and the smaller kingdoms of Arabia.

"My people," said the Emir of Transjordania, "stand behind our democratic allies to the end."

"Our sympathies go out to Great Britain in this war against the evil forces of Nazidom, and as a sign of our sympathy we wish to give £30,000 to the Government," said the Sheikh of Bahrein.

The Sultan of Oman called on his 55,000 subjects to do all that might be required of them, while the rulers of Koweit and Dabai offered "all our resources to achieve an early victory."

The Egyptian Waafd had expressed its confidence in the "unity of the whole Moslem world" behind the Western Democracies. That unity was soon reflected on behalf of seven million Indian Moslems by their leader, the Aga Khan. Immediately before offering

An Empire Answers

the personal services of himself and his son he declared it "the duty of all Moslems to co-operate heart and soul for the success of His Majesty the King Emperor."

His loyalty was echoed by every ruling prince in India without a single exception; some offering men, some money, and some both.

It is true that among the Congress leaders of Hindu Nationalism one only urged that "whatever support was given to Britain should be given unconditionally."

But that one was Mahatma Gandhi.

But the others saw in the war a chance, not to oppose Britain, it is true, but to further their cause, to demand that their support would be repaid with a more generous measure of self-government when the war was ended. Yet they were profuse in their desire "to show the greatest consideration for the English"— since, as Pandit Nehru, the most extreme of them put it, "India's freedom will not be worth many days' purchase if Nazism should dominate the world."

Among the native races of the African continent there were no dissentients from the common cause.

British rule had certainly not been perfect in all the African colonies, still less had British colonisation.

But the natives had a very clear idea of the sort of alternative that German rule provided. Memories in the desert last long. Men's minds still went back along the West Coast to the days when the Herero fought Germany for his right to exist, and lost it when the Imperial Governor von Trotha proclaimed "that every Herero with or without a rifle, with or without cattle, shall be shot," and when the remnants of the Herero people were rounded up in the Omaheke desert, and left to die there. Four years' war from 1903-1907 had reduced the Herero people from 70,000 to 30,000. That was under the Kaiser. Hitler promised to be still harsher. Had he not said that the "nigger should be confined to slave tasks." His theories of race and colour, of superior and helot were familiar to both East and West Coast chiefs. Some, too, were aware of the Nazi concept that lumped niggers, Jews and monkeys on the lowest rung of that ladder, whose summit was occupied by the Nordic Germans.

Among the first volunteers in Tanganyika Territory were many veterans of the Maji-Maji war against the Germans in 1904.

Before the first week of the war had ended the common native greeting in the Territory was "*Kwa Mfalfame Weto.*"—"For Our King."

All through the Rhodesias, Kenya, Nyasaland, Nigeria, and the West Coast provinces chiefs and elders travelled hundreds of miles down the native trails to offer fighters and porters to the Great White King. The intensity of native feeling was summed up in the resolution of the Bulawayo Bantus pledging themselves to be faithful "even if the Heavens fall," and in the unanimous declaration of the Basuto Chieftains, "We are the same people as of old. Our King is at war and so are we." "If it comes to the worst," said the Paramount Chief of Accra, "I will take my sandals off and walk barefoot with the British soldiers right into the firing line."

The Nazis had counted so much on rebellion in the Colonies against Britain, and they had seen instead the very deserts rise to mock their hopes.

But they still had their tenth legion—the German-born colonists. The third Reich had sought to brand their hearts with the sign of the swastika. She had striven to envelop them like Brunhilde with a sacred flame which Hitler alone could still.

What happened to them?

Although the German-born colonists formed a powerful block in their former colonies of South-West Africa and Tanganyika territory there was no attempt at resistance in either province. A few irreconcilables fled tamely over the Tanganyika borders. But the authorities were agreeably surprised at the number of Germans who volunteered their services. At Swakapmund in South-West Africa, a city three-quarters German, more than half the population had registered for defence within 24 hours.

Truly Hitler, reading through his reports, must have wondered what kind of power it was that he had challenged when he went to war against the British Empire.

But the point of balance of the African Continent below the Sahara, was, of course, the Union of South Africa. The Afrikander population was rather more than 60 per cent of the whole. It was only in Natal and parts of the Cape Province that the British were a majority. Among the Afrikanders—we knew them as the Boers—were still many who had fought bitterly and bravely against the tide of British conquest at the beginning of the century.

To have fought on the Boer side was almost as essential to success in public life in South Africa in the nineteen thirties as was service with the Federal Army to a politician in the United States in the third quarter of the nineteenth century.

Both the principal leaders, Generals Hertzog and

Smuts, enjoyed that distinction. General Smuts had actually led the Cape Forces in the latter stages of the struggle.

But General Smuts had fought for Britain in 1914. He had commanded the army which conquered South-West Africa, and although he protested wisely and with vision against the severity of the peace terms at Versailles and often questioned the sincerity of post-war British Governments to the League of Nations ideal, his devotion to the Empire remained unshaken.

General Hertzog took a different line. When the war of 1939 broke out he advocated nothing more than a benevolent neutrality. General Hertzog's caution was opposed by the Imperial loyalty of General Smuts, who carried first the Cabinet and then the Parliament. Hertzog fell. Smuts was carried to the Premiership on the cry of "Side by side with Britain."

In the country feeling ran high for General Smuts. The very existence of a minority in favour of neutrality served to strengthen the intensity of feeling. There were ugly demonstrations against German-owned shops. The Johannesburg police were compelled to use tear gas. The city opened a fund to provide a free gift of one million pounds' worth of food for Great Britain. Port Elizabeth and East London subscribed funds to build a destroyer, and it was eloquent of the trend in Union opinion that one of General Hertzog's most prominent supporters, Colonel Deneys Reitz, who had once chosen a self-imposed exile in Madagascar rather than live in a British-ruled South Africa, now ranged himself with General Smuts.

"I fight for Britain because of the great generosity

An Empire Answers

she has shown my people whom she conquered," he said when he came to London a few weeks later.

All the islands of the Mediterranean, the West and East Indies, put themselves into a state of active defence. But of all the evidence of loyalty with which Britain was overwhelmed in the early days of war, perhaps the least expected, was the adhesion of the Jamaican agitator Bustamente.

About the Commonwealth of Australia there were never any doubts, and she lost no time in declaring herself.

The Prime Minister, Mr. Menzies, has said "that if Britain went to war she would not go alone." And when, in fact, Britain did go to war Australia was with her from the first day.

"We have no hatred for the German people in our hearts," Mr. Menzies declared. "What we hate and mean to crush is the dominating power which has led the German people to this disastrous crime."

The Commonwealth war effort was four times as great as in 1914. There were eighty thousand militia under arms, there was the 6th Division, twenty thousand strong, mobilized for service at home or abroad. And there was the offer of the Australian Expeditionary Air Force, six squadrons strong, for service on the Western Front.

New Zealand immediately offered an infantry division to go wherever the British Commander-in-Chief directed. She called, too, for nine hundred airmen to come forward for service overseas. Within the month the division was enrolled.

Even the native Maoris, though they, too, were on the list of Britain's former enemies, raised their own volunteer battalion. And the call for nine hundred airmen was answered by two thousand. That was only a beginning. Every year 1,300 airmen were promised by the remote Dominion, perhaps the most essentially British of them all. She entered the struggle, in her Prime Minister's words, "both with gratitude for the past, and with confidence in the future. . . . We range ourselves fearlessly behind Britain. Where she goes, we go, and we stand where she stands."

No Dominion in the British Empire comes under so powerful, even if so friendly, an alien influence as Canada.

The immense pressure of the neighbouring republic of the United States, with its more than a hundred million inhabitants, is seen in every exterior aspect of Canadian life. With an acumen which might have been copied by the City of London, American finance has made itself the dominating force in Canadian industrial and mineral development.

As I have said before, President Roosevelt guaranteed the integrity of Canada in 1938.

With the practical cessation of British emigration after the end of the last war, and with the larger families of the French Canadians, the preponderance of British-bred stock became less and less.

European communities were created in the Western Provinces with their own languages and their own little newspapers. Truly, a Canadian anxious to maintain the Imperial connections might have faced with some apprehension the challenge that would come with a second world war.

Mr. Mackenzie King, the Prime Minister, went no further in advance than to say that if hostilities should break out, Canada would be legally at war. The extent of her participation, however, would be determined after the outbreak by the Canadian Parliament. Whether he should have gone further or not will always be a point of debate in Canada itself.

On every hand he was attacked and criticized, and, I must confess, that my own was one of the voices that joined in those attacks.

After war was declared the Canadian Parliament was summoned to Ottawa to determine its part. I wish that I could have been there to have heard one speech—that of the Hon. Ernest Lapointe, the Member for East Quebec, holding the portfolio of Minister of Justice. In the last war he had been counted 'against'—certainly against conscription and partly against British participation. The latter part of that may not have been so, but such was the value that his countrymen put upon his action at that time.

On September 9th of this year he rose in his place. The whole House listened in tense silence, for it was obvious that the words he would utter must have a profound influence upon the decision to be taken. It was felt that when he spoke it would be for French Canada. Quietly and soberly he reviewed the situation which had brought Great Britain to war. He recalled his hopes for the League of Nations, and declared:

"I hate war with all my heart and conscience." He paused, and then added these words, "But devotion to peace does not mean ignorance or blindness. . . . England has worked for peace. I know it. It is a base calumny to say that England is responsible for anything that has led to the present conflict. France has worked continually for peace, and it is a slander to say that France is responsible in any way for the conflict. These nations have gone so far in their efforts to preserve peace that they have been the subject of strong and bitter criticism on the part of many people in their respective countries because of what was called with derision the 'appeasement' policy.... A proposal has been made in some newspapers and at meetings which have been heard during the last few days that I am almost ashamed to refer to it. Some say 'Let volunteers go from Canada if they wish, but let England pay for them, or let those who take the initiative in organizing regiments pay the cost.' They say 'Go, but let England bear the cost or pay for it yourselves. You may give your life, you may shed your blood, but your country refuses to pay the expense incidental to your sacrifice.' I am too proud and too conscious of Canadian dignity to discuss such a proposal. Canadians will never be mercenaries paid by any country—even by Britain."

Then he came to the end of his speech.

Moved by a profound emotion which swept the whole Chamber, he said:

"I desire to conclude my remarks by referring to what was said by our gracious Queen at Halifax when she was leaving Canada to return to the homeland. Her words in French went to the heart of every man, woman and child in my Province. She said, "*Que Dieu benisse le Canada.*' God bless Canada! Yes, God bless Canada! God save Canada! God save Canada's honour, Canada's soul, Canada's dignity, Canada's conscience!

"God give Canadians the light which will indicate to them where their duty lies in this hour of trial so that our children and our children's children may inherit a land where freedom and peace shall prevail, where our social, political and religious institutions may be secure and from which the tyrannical doctrines of Nazism and Communism are forever banished. Yes, God bless Canada. God bless our Queen. God bless our King."

There was no division. Under the leadership of Mr. Mackenzie King a united parliament for a united Dominion declared Canada to be at the side of Britain until victory was assured.

The Empire story was complete.

Chapter VI

The Great Neutral

EARLY IN THE SUMMER OF 1939, PRESIdent Roosevelt's plan to amend the Neutrality Act was blocked. When the war had been in progress for two months it was carried.

The issue was a simple enough one. In America's desire to maintain her historic policy of avoiding foreign entanglements, she had passed a law by which no armaments or war supplies could be sold to any belligerent nation. It is easy to see the good intention behind it, and the degree of idealism which always plays such a big part in American legislation. Unfortunately, that policy became a direct encouragement to aggression. No matter how great its sympathies with the weaker nation, the U.S.A. could not export anything more tangible than goodwill.

So President Roosevelt decided to amend it. How far did the refusal of Congress to carry out his wishes influence Hitler in going to war?

That may seem an extreme question, but one must remember that the German Government is composed of men who are almost completely ignorant of the outside world. For any foreigner the ways of Washington are difficult enough. No one can dogmatize upon it, but I think it possible that in those days when storms were raging in Hitler's brain, when he was trying to reach a decision out of the tempestuous upheaval of his emotions, the action of the American

The Great Neutral

Parliament may have played some part. The sequel must be equally true. When, in late October 1939, the amendment was carried, thus definitely favouring the Allied cause, I have no doubt at all that Hitler suffered an intense sense of discouragement. Unfortunately, the war had already begun.

America's historic desire is to remain isolated from Europe. America's passionate interest is in everything European. America tries to draw the ocean about her like a skirt, and to say that Europe is no concern of hers. Yet nothing that America does fails to have its influence on the Old World, just as everything in Europe has its repercussions in the United States.

And of all European nations, the one which is closest to America, both physically and spiritually, is Great Britain.

The story of Anglo-American relations since the war is a strange one. In many ways it is a most unhappy story.

There is no use denying the fact that for the two or three years preceding the present war, the feeling of America towards Great Britain grew steadily cooler. And since the feelings of nations are not greatly different from those of individuals, there has been a corresponding coolness in the attitude of Britain herself. Nothing in modern history is more regrettable, and unless careful and sympathetic thought is given to the problem, the harm that it is doing may extend into the years ahead.

No one could blame the people of the United States for feeling disillusioned after the Great War. They had come into the conflict, as America always has done, with an immense, surging idealism. The great

Republic of the New World was created out of resentment against injustice. When, later, she had her civil war, those terrible four years of incredible fortitude and unbelievable bravery, it was idealism that supplied the driving force. When, in 1917, the young men of America stormed across the ocean to the assistance of the Allies, it was to free the world of an intolerable militaristic tyranny.

No mistake is greater than to imagine that America is actuated by basically selfish motives. Of all people Americans are the most emotional, the most idealistic, and, tragically, of all great peoples they are the most persistently ill-informed on world events.

Once they had re-entered Europe as they did in 1917, they could never withdraw. The world had narrowed until its oceans had become lakes, and its lakes mere ponds. Communications and transport in the urgency of war had advanced until the globe was shrunk like a deflated balloon.

But when a nation is given to quick emotionalism it is also given to swift disillusionment. Versailles offended the Americans with its return to power politics. Yet their President had given to unhappy Europe the one practical thing which alone could have justified the awful sacrifices of the war. The League of Nations was a wonderful ideal. With America as its presiding genius we would undoubtedly have seen to-day a world of immense advancement with war an ugly anachronism of the past. Yet I can recall with painful clarity that scene in St. James's Palace in 1920 when the League held its first Assembly in London. In the great art gallery of the palace I heard a Japanese Minister in broken English pleading for Polish minori-

The Great Neutral

ties, I heard M. Bourgeois of France enunciating an idealism which would have broken down frontiers. But I also heard Arthur Balfour apologizing for the empty chair at the table. The nation which had given the ideal to the world had withdrawn. Summon what argument you like, that was a cruel blow to civilization and to the hopes of men.

Previously it had been promised that the U.S.A., along with Britain, would guarantee the integrity of France. But Congress said no. The internal campaign against President Wilson had reached its climax, and the elected representatives of the United States were determined to wipe out every implication of his immense efforts on behalf of humanity.

The burden of reconstructing Europe was left to Great Britain. If we did it badly, who is there to say that the burden was a fair one?

In Great Britain, however, there was also a basic change of policy, despite her loyalty to the League. With that instinct for the centuries which is in the very soil of England, it was felt that the future of the world lay in the close understanding of the English-speaking peoples. Therefore everything possible was done to bring about that objective. To please Washington, and to some extent Ottawa, we broke with our loyal ally, Japan. To please Washington we sent Mr. Baldwin there, who made that incredible settlement of the American debt. It was a reproach alike to him and to those who drew it up. To placate Irish-American opinion we created the Free State, and gambled on the future. When America was engaged in her strange experiment of Prohibition we conceded the three-mile limit, and extended it to twelve to help the U.S. Government to control the gun-running that was going on. When President Hoover asked that we should forgive Germany her reparations in order to bring about a better economic order of things we did so, although our debt to America remained uncancelled.

Never has a great country more persistently endeavoured to create a cordial understanding with another than did Britain in those post-war years. Unfortunately the various British Governments made one great psychological mistake. When the impossible terms of the Baldwin settlement brought a halt to the payments of the war debt, they were never resumed, except by a token payment which meant nothing.

The result was deplorable, and more than anything else laid the foundation of the coolness which has characterized the last three years. The case for the cancellation of the debt was overwhelming. When America came into the war in 1917, she did so as a full ally. But she was not ready. She had neither the trained men nor the equipment. When, a year later, her full force began to be felt in France, it undoubtedly turned the scales. But in the year that she was preparing, tens of thousands of young Britons and Frenchmen died holding the line.

America demanded the repayment of her dollars. We could not demand the return of the dead. Yet America, in strict logic, should have valued in dollars and cents the lives of those who held the line, and she should have applied it as a contra account. The mere thought of such a transaction is sickening. The human soul revolts against it at once. But unless the American Government was willing to value the dead, she was

The Great Neutral

not in a position to insist upon the value of her dollars.

Nevertheless, in spite of Britain's adjustments, America maintained that the debt was due to her. That being so, we should have paid. The normal American citizen, quite unable to follow the logic of the case, came to look upon Britain as a defaulter. I have heard the charge a thousand times in my many visits to the United States, and it never grew easier to bear with repetition.

Even then that might not have poisoned the good relations of the two countries if an entirely new phenomenon had not arisen with the growth of the European dictatorships.

As I have said, the Americans are quick in their sympathies, and when Abyssinia was invaded by Italy they felt that Britain should have done something about it. Later on, this feeling grew doubly strong when Austria, Republican Spain, and Czechoslovakia went down to destruction.

The interest of Americans in Europe had reached fever-heat. As the law of supply and demand is quickly adjusted in the Republic, there developed almost over-night a strange army of foreign correspondents who crossed to Europe to see the tragedy at first hand. They all wrote books about it, and most of the books were of one kind. In sneering, contemptuous words they charged Great Britain with standing by, and even conniving at the murder of liberty in Europe.

The American café-to-crisis correspondents were not the only ones. British correspondents like Mr. Douglas Reed and Mr. G. E. R. Gedye joined in the attack with their books, and because of their British nationality did immeasurable harm in inflaming American opinion against us. The great bulk of American newspapers were perfectly fair. There were famous newspapers like the *New York Times*, the *Herald-Tribune*, the *New York Sun*, and the *Washington Post*, which set themselves out to put the British case with friendliness and absolute fairness.

On the other hand, there had grown up in the U.S.A. that type of "the news behind the news" publication which prospered so exceedingly in the unhappy months preceding the abdication of King Edward VIII. These journals fastened upon Mr. Chamberlain as their victim. One story after another was published with the utmost minutiae of detail proving that Mr. Chamberlain was a tool in the hands of the Cliveden set, a mere cypher under the domination of Mr. Montagu Norman, a pawn in the hands of the aristocracy, or a dithering ex-Lord Mayor of Birmingham completely out of his depth.

Those stories did for a while, but appetite grows with what it feeds upon. The readers wanted stronger meat—and the supply rose to meet the demand.

There are two skilful journalists named Drew Pearson and Robert Allen, who write a daily syndicated political column called the 'Washington Merry-go-Round.' This appears, I should think, in at least 150 representative American newspapers. One day, these gentlemen decided to publish the full truth about the British Prime Minister. They said that he was the biggest shareholder in Imperial Chemicals, and through that enormous corporation controlled a large section of the German armament industry. Thus everything

The Great Neutral

was made clear. In order to add to his already stupendous millions, Mr. Chamberlain was in favour of constant war scares to stimulate armament production, but he intended to avoid war itself because that might bring in some bad debts, and so end the demand for armaments. Some fifty or sixty cuttings of this outrageous column were sent to me from the United States and Canada. Decent people asked if I would tell them if it were true. Others hoped that I could do something to refute the libel.

I made enquiries at No. 10, Downing Street, and was told that Mr. Chamberlain, although he, too, had received many clippings, intended to do nothing about it. I called up my old friend, Lord McGowan, the Chairman of Imperial Chemicals, but he said that he must follow the attitude of the Prime Minister. I went to see Mr. Joseph Kennedy, the American Ambassador, one of the greatest men that ever entered the world of diplomacy. Mr. Kennedy looked at the document, and his face was a study.

"What can be done about it?" he asked sadly. "Not long ago I gave an interview in America which was of a depressing character, for it seemed to me then that war was inevitable. I have just read in one of our own newspapers over there that I cleared up four million dollars by going 'Bear' in the market the day before. It is heartbreaking, but how can public men reply to charges like these?"

I don't know the answer myself, but human nature which retains its suspicions through the centuries could not understand the British Premier's silence. The man who is accused and does not reply is already three parts guilty. In desperation, and without consulting anyone in the Government, I myself wrote to Messrs. Drew Pearson and Robert Allen in Washington. Because I believe that this aspect of Anglo-American relations is of more than passing importance, I take the liberty of quoting from my letter :

"Gentlemen,

"I trust that you will not resent this letter. It is written as one newspaper man to two other newspaper men. Merely to establish my credentials, I was for some years Editor of the *Daily Express*, and am now Editorial Adviser to Lord Kemsley's Allied Group. I am also a member of the British House of Commons, but that does not matter very much at the moment.

"There is not very much difference between newspaper men the world over. They are basically honest, financially improvident, and cynically idealistic. Beneath everything else there is an essential decency which does not always come out in their work, but exists in their private relationships.

"A few weeks ago in your interesting and skilful column you pictured Mr. Neville Chamberlain as a powerful figure in the world of armaments and directly interested in various subsidiary German armament firms. You gave the impression that Mr. Chamberlain was the dominating shareholder in Imperial Chemicals, and that his foreign policy was trimmed to suit his financial advantage.

"I do not believe that you would willingly publish something that is not only completely but grotesquely untrue. Mr. Chamberlain has many enemies in England, and some of them are very

The Great Neutral

bitter, but such a charge as you have made would not be accepted by any of them for a moment. No country is without its crooks, and we have some very good ones over here, but British public life is absolutely clear of even a suspicion of personal dishonesty. Not only does a politician make no money out of being in the House of Commons, but the system would not allow him to do it, even if he wanted to. There is no patronage. No politician has anything to do with appointments. Finally, there is the tradition that men in public life sacrifice their financial interests rather than enhance them. I am not trying to paint a glowing picture. I am merely telling you what is simply the truth. Neville Chamberlain is a poor man. I would be greatly surprised if the income from his investments exceeds £2,000 a year. His brother, Austen, had to give up his small country cottage because his income would not permit the expense.

"Mr. Chamberlain can be criticized from many angles, but to attribute to him the character of a grafter is to besmirch the person who makes so false and foolish a charge.

"I know that a daily column does not give its authors very much time to investigate the story upon which they base their paragraphs. At any rate, I hope you will not resent this letter. It is written with complete sincerity on my part, and I do not even ask for any retraction on your part. It is just a genuine dislike of seeing two decent journalists publishing something that is not worthy of them. . . ."

Men, Martyrs and Mountebanks

In the course of time I received a most cordial and friendly letter from the authors of the column. They said they certainly had no intention of being unfair to Mr. Chamberlain, and were very glad indeed that I had taken the trouble to write to them. They agreed that probably they had not investigated the story fully enough, and again thanked me. Nothing could exceed the courtesy of their reply, or its evident sincerity, but had I written to them to say that they had accused Mr. Chamberlain of wearing a bowler instead of a top hat their acknowledgment could only have been in the same terms. They had made an infamous and despicable charge against a great statesman, against the head of a friendly country. I have no means of checking it, but I do not believe that they have made any attempt in their column to retract what they said.

But we must not imagine that this persistent campaign of defamation was carried on by newspaper correspondents alone. We supplied powerful help from this country. Mr. H. G. Wells used his pen to tell the American public that the British Government was contemptible. British renegades like Boake Carter caught the ear of the American public, and made substantial rewards on the radio and in the Press by spreading this calumny against Great Britain. No wonder the American people believed that Britain's sun had declined, and that she had entered the twilight of the gods.

We did nothing to counteract it. The policy of 'do nothing, say nothing' was in full force both in London and at our Embassy in Washington. So strong was the anti-British campaign that even certain refugees to whom we had shown the greatest courtesy and consideration, joined in.

When I was in North America early in the August preceding the war, I picked up a magazine in which Emil Ludwig, the biographer, had a double page comparing Stalin with Chamberlain. There was no sneer too cheap for the British Prime Minister, there was no compliment too florid for the Russian Dictator. Yet I can remember the author coming to London after he had left Germany and receiving not only bread and wine, but being given that psychological encouragement which he needed so badly at the time. Colonel Lindbergh's outburst against us when the war was on received more publicity than it deserved. He, as well as General Johnson, who wrote that in Europe we were simply a lot of mad dogs, were carrying on a tradition that was soundly established. But of all the instruments of anti-British propaganda, nothing was so persistent or so effective as the *Saturday Evening Post*. Because its editorials were written with more restraint of language, they probably had all the greater effect. Continuously and unfairly they urged the case against this country.

Perhaps the wonder is that there remains in America so much kindly and friendly feeling towards us. It was in July of 1939 that a number of American editors flew across in the *Clipper*. I helped to entertain some of them, and also met them at Lord Beaverbrook's party. They were astonished to find a Britain completely resolute and ready for war. They expressed their admiration with a frankness that was moving. Some of them have since sent me copies of their newspapers, in which they told the story of Britain in splendid and glowing terms. Nowhere is there greater sincerity of purpose in journalism than in the United States. The editors want to be accurate, and they want to be fair in what they portray, but what could they do against the flood of ill-report which flowed all about them?

What is going to happen now? No one can deny that the friendship and understanding of the English-speaking peoples has been clouded by the course of events, and I think it is only right that I should try to summarize what, in my opinion, is the feeling of Britain towards the United States:

The British believe instinctively and profoundly in the necessity of the English-speaking peoples going forward into the future side by side.

The British realize with profound thankfulness that whatever may happen there can never again be war between Great Britain and America.

The British recognize with gratitude that the civilization of America is in itself an immense and powerful factor for peace.

But—

The British people cannot understand why America has constituted herself the prosecuting counsel, judge and jury, with no responsibility for implementing the verdict. When Czechoslovakia was dismembered at Munich America cried out that the little Republic had been sold down the river. When, following Von Rath's assassination, the Nazi scum were turned loose upon the Jews in Germany, the heat of America's anger could be felt across the Atlantic. When the Germans marched into Prague the anger of America knew no bounds, and once more Britain was accused of being too cowardly to fight.

The Great Neutral

Now, Britain and France have gone to war. We are out to end the scheme of things by which smaller countries can be murdered in broad daylight, and America, which led the anger, grows cold and says it is no direct concern of hers.

The policy of isolation is one that can be understood. To remain outside the conflicts of Europe may well be the proper course of the American Government, and certainly it is a matter for Washington alone to decide. But to span within the space of a few months the surging of righteous anger because we did not fight and the cold chill of apparent indifference when we did fight is something which puzzles the British as they look across the sea.

America cannot shed responsibility for the Europe of to-day. As the world's creditor and as the creator of super tariffs she is not in a position to claim that the deterioration of European economy was entirely the fault of the countries of the Old World. At any time in the last three years America could have taken her stand by the side of Britain, and this war would never have happened. America is too great, too powerful, too dominating a factor in civilization to stand aside. Neither by the "significance nor the insignificance" of her actions can she avoid influencing the destiny of the world.

It is true that the republic of the United States of America was created out of resentment against injustice, but her birth would have been inevitable in any case. That country, with its double gateways of the oceans and the inherent character of its people, was destined to play a mighty part in human history.

Because of the American revolution, the revolution

in France had to be. From the very beginning a policy of isolation was impossible.

Some day the English-speaking peoples must go forward together. With France and such other nations as are peace-minded they must create a new order of life for mankind.

There is no other way.

Chapter VII

Moonlight Over Bucharest

WHEN THE MOON SHINES ON BUCHAREST and the gipsy orchestras play in the open-air cafés, there is romance in the air. When the lightning strikes and the thunder echoes in the distant mountains of Sinaia, there is fear in Bucharest.

One day in June in the spring of 1938 I went to King Carol's palace. The palace is so clean, so white, so modern, that it was almost like a super clinic in a Hollywood film. There were fine paintings on the walls, for Carol has an eye for beauty as well as for value. The attendants were in white uniforms as spotless as the shining floors. The King himself was in white, for in Bucharest the days in June are warm.

A week before, the King had abolished Parliament, and sentenced Codreanu with the other leaders of the Iron Guard to ten years' imprisonment. This Hitler-inspired and German-financed organization of terrorism had risen to such power that the collapse of the existing administration had left the door open for them to form a government.

But they had not reckoned with the King. For years this Hohenzollern had filled the newspapers of the world with his romantic exploits. The reading public of Britain and America knew all about Carol and Mme. Lupescu and nothing whatever about Rumania.

Codreanu inflamed the youth of his country. They

say he had consumption, which may or may not be true. He looked and carried himself like a film star revolutionary. He had glamour, he had good looks, he had fire and melancholy, and courage of a kind. When M. Duca, the then Prime Minister, had tried to put down the Iron Guard movement they waited for him at the railway station at Sinaia. Rumania could boast of many faults, but political assassination was not one. It was the Hitler technique which introduced it when Duca's body was riddled by the revolvers of Germany's Fifth Column in Rumania.

"Is this a popular thing you have done," I asked the King, "in sentencing Codreanu to ten years?"

"Not popular," the King answered, "and not unpopular. The fellow is no good. He is not even second-rate. He is a wretched creature, and prison is the place for him. I am determined that we shall have order."

A puzzling yet attractive personality, this Balkan king. His English is facile, although his accent is guttural, as bespeaks his German origin. His eyes have an excited gleam to them, strangely at variance with the clarity of his thoughts. He looked at the gathering menace of events without false optimism or despair. Perhaps he felt that he might be the last of the Balkan kings.

"What is your attitude towards Germany?" I asked.

"I am neither anti-German nor pro-German," he answered. "But I am pro-Rumanian. There are many things I like about the Germans. As business men they are naturally honest. Their instinct is to go through with a contract, even if it does not pay. They show great interest in my country. I wish that England would show a little interest, too. Your instinct, of course, in England, is always to look from London to Calcutta and not to care what happens between. But something may get on the line between London and Calcutta. It is even possible that the independent existence of Rumania could be classed as a British interest."

That afternoon M. Duca, the brother of the murdered Premier, took me to a race meeting which was being held in honour of the eighth anniversary of the king's return from exile. M. Duca was Chief Steward and was good enough to give me such excellent advice that I was able to back every winner but one. He himself, of course, made no bets.

"You have done well," he said with a smile. "What a pity you cannot take the money out of the country." Next day, M. Tilea, now the distinguished Rumanian Minister to London, gave a luncheon for me. He pointed to the end of the table, where a man was sitting with a dark monocle over one eye. It was a remarkable face. Alert, yet calm. A face of character and strength, yet with a strange suggestion of sadness.

"That is Calinescu. He is the coming man," said M. Tilea. That night M. Gafencu, the owner of the Bucharest newspaper *Timpul,* gave a dinner party in his lovely home. There were coloured lights in the trees of his garden, and there was beauty both in the eyes of the women and in the moon that hovered in the skies.

"I take no part in politics now," said the goodlooking Gafencu. "A newspaper proprietor has no time except for his newspaper."

Men, Martyrs and Mountebanks

As is its habit, July followed June and gave way, in turn, to August. Berchtesgaden, Godesberg, Munich! The little Republic of Czechoslovakia lay helpless and dismembered in the path of the conqueror. Poland snatched Teschen, Hungary staked her claim. The skies over Bucharest were dark and threatening.

A new figure emerged. The newspaper proprietor, Gafencu, took on the most difficult task in the Balkans, Foreign Minister for Rumania. His grandfather was a Scot, which accounted for much. There are not many blondes in Rumania of either sex. He had fought in the Rumanian Air Force against the Germans, and so bravely that the British decorated him with the Military Cross. There was dignity and there was distinction in this tall, courteous ex-airman, ex-journalist, and now Foreign Minister. He began his round of the small countries. He went to Yugo-slavia, to Turkey, to Bulgaria. Wherever he went he sounded the warning. "The Balkans must unite, or all of us are lost."

At the end of the year King Carol prepared to visit London.

"I leave the security of the State in your hands," he said to the Home Secretary of his government. It was M. Calinescu, the man with the dark monocle over his eye and the face that had a touch of sadness.

M. Gafencu accompanied the King to London. So did M. Tilea, who was as yet a private citizen.

I was delighted to renew acquaintance with them both, and King Carol, with the usual memory of a monarch, was good enough to recall my visit to Bucharest. From London the King went to Berlin, accompanied by his stalwart son, Prince Michael. Ostensibly the visit was to see relatives, but there was also an invitation from the German Fuehrer. Hitler asked the Rumanian monarch to bring his son to Berchtesgaden to see the man who had succeeded the Hohenzollern dynasty. It is now possible to reveal what happened.

Hitler was ill at ease, for his contacts with royalty had been few. Notoriously a man of slight conversational gifts, and not inclined to deliver one of his oratorical performances of political shrieking, his attempts to make the interview pleasant were well meant but not too successful.

King Carol lit a cigarette without asking. So did Michael. Hitler, who never invites a guest to smoke and who cannot bear it, said nothing. But the pleasantness of his demeanour took a sudden change.

"Will you answer me a question?" he said.

"What is it?" asked Carol.

"Will you let the Russians come through Rumania?"

Carol flicked the ash from his cigarette.

"You have asked me one question," he said. "May I, in turn, ask you two?"

Hitler made a gesture of acquiescence.

"Do you intend," asked the King, "to support Codreanu, and do you intend to interfere with the German minority in Rumania?"

For a moment it seemed as if Hitler was going to resent what was said. Then he changed his mind and, speaking in tones of the greatest possible reasonableness, he said:

"I have no desire to interfere with the internal government of your country, and I am not going to support Codreanu. Nevertheless, you must see the delicacy of my position. Codreanu made himself my follower and chief supporter in Rumania. You can understand that it is a matter of distress to me that he is in prison. I ask you to accept my assurance that I am not interested in his political activities, because of my irrevocable decision never to interfere in any way with your country. Therefore, I would be very much obliged if you would release Codreanu and the other leaders of the Iron Guard, and take them away from the prison in which they are incarcerated. You will appreciate that I make this only as a request."

There was a silence, and the two men looked at each other. Carol's eyes, no doubt, had that curious gleam, and by that time Hitler's eyes were probably smouldering. The interview drew to its close.

"You have not answered my question," said Hitler. "Do you intend to let the Russians come through?"

"No," said Carol.

The two Hohenzollerns took their leave of the ex-sign painter of Austria. But strange coincidences happen in international events. From the time that King Carol had left Bucharest to visit London, the Iron Guard had reappeared, and outrages were the order of the day and night. At the very hour that they were talking to Hitler, murder was stalking the streets of Bucharest. The leader was in prison, but his example lived on.

King Carol concluded his German visit, and prepared to leave for home. Far off in Rumania the wardens appeared at the cells occupied by Codreanu and the thirteen other leaders of the Iron Guard.

"You are going to be moved," they said. The prisoners were taken away in a lorry with a strong military escort. Going through a deserted wood they were ambushed. According to the official statement issued that night, Codreanu and all his colleagues were killed in trying to escape. It must have been a one-sided struggle. Not a single soldier was wounded. And, stranger still, although the ground was wet, those who had taken part in the ambush left no footsteps. The bodies were buried, and the military escort returned to duty.

When the King reached Bucharest, he sent for Calinescu.

"Your Majesty," said the Home Secretary, "I have maintained order in your realm."

Again, as is the habit of the seasons, spring came to Europe. A little early, perhaps, for perfect weather, the Nazis went for a walk—to Prague. The tragedy of Czechoslovakia was complete.

Then came the great surprise. Britain, that decrepit, milk-fed lion, was showing its teeth. With insufferable insolence it had spread its protecting paw over Poland. Another paw rested upon Rumania. Hitler's fury mounted to fever-heat. He was just about to celebrate his fiftieth birthday, and England was threatening to spoil the whole affair.

"I wish to see this fellow Gafencu," said Hitler to Ribbentrop. So Gafencu journeyed to Berchtesgaden and sat in the same seat as Schuschnigg had done. Two days later he came to London, and at dinner we again renewed our friendship of the year before. The interview with Hitler had been an interesting one. Goering took part in it, and there had been a strange contrast at first in the manner of the two Nazi leaders. It was Goering who roared and blustered. It was Hitler who was calm and friendly.

"Why have you signed a defensive pact with England?" asked Hitler.

"Yes, why?" demanded Goering. "You know that she could do nothing to help you. You would be overrun and crushed before a single British soldier could go to your assistance."

"That is probably true," said Gafencu.

Goering turned angrily upon him. "Then why did you do it?" he roared.

Gafencu, whose courtesy never leaves him, made a slight inclination of his head.

"The British guarantee to a small nation," he said, "is useful when a war is over."

Hitler's shoulders slumped as if with fatigue. Goering snorted angrily, but said nothing.

This cursed legend that Britain always won the last battle. *Gott strafe England.* Yes. *Gott strafe England.*

"What were you before you were a diplomat?" asked Goering.

"A newspaper man," answered Gafencu. "But before that I was an airman, and had the honour of fighting against the forces of Your Excellency."

Goering went out. He had had enough.

Hitler took over. Suddenly the listless form of the Fuehrer came to life. Almost leaping to his feet, and with the lightning flashing from his eyes, he started one of his famous tirades. With words that tumbled over each other he shrieked of the horrors which Britain and France would undergo if they were fools enough to bring about a war.

"There will not be a town or city in England or France," he cried, "that will not be bombed out of existence. There will be nothing left. They will be countries of the dead. The fools ! They have no idea of the horrors that would come upon them."

With his face twitching, the Fuehrer threw himself into the chair again. All his vitality had gone as suddenly as it had burst into flame.

"And if we fight," he said, with his eyes staring into space, "whom do we fight for ? . . . *For Moscow.*"

The last two words came with a hiss of hatred. That mood passed, and Hitler, once more amiable and gentle, said that he would not be happy unless M. Gafencu came to his birthday celebrations in Berlin. Accordingly, on the morning of that interesting occasion, a motor-car arrived at Gafencu's hotel, and took him to the platform where all the officials were waiting. Then he saw the place reserved for him. It was between Seyss Inquart, the man who had sold Austria, and Dr. Hacha, the President of the Czechs, who had meekly gone in March to Hitler to ask him to invade his country.

"You will forgive me," M. Gafencu said to his escorting officer, "but I have forgotten something. I must go back to my hotel."

The fiftieth celebration of the Fuehrer's birthday took place without the presence of Rumania's Foreign Minister.

September, 1939—and war.

Poland disappears like a candle caught in a gale. Russia pours its red stream into Europe. Hitler prostrates himself before Stalin, and touches his brow to the ground three times. . . . "*For Moscow.*"

So swiftly had his prophecy come true.

September is a lovely month in Rumania. So thought M. Calinescu, now Prime Minister, as he drove from his house towards his office early in the afternoon.

It was by the bridge at Dembovitza that his car was blocked, and a fusillade of bullets shattered the air.

He fell forward dead, this man with a dark monocle over one eye and the face that was curiously sad.

King Carol had lost his man of iron, but he himself is no king of straw. The assassins were arrested and taken to the spot of their crime. There they were shot and there the bodies were left lying on the ground for all to take warning from their fate. All night long the pistols rang out as the law avenged itself for the second Prime Minister to go down before the subsidised bullets of Adolf Hitler.

There is no lovelier September than that in Bucharest and in that week the skies were clear, and there was a shimmering beauty everywhere.

Many people had remarked, however, how large the star Mars had been, and how red.

Chapter VIII

Stalin Plays His Hand

MAN HAS SOMETIMES CHOSEN STRANGE objects to adore.

The ancient Egyptians used to adore crocodiles.

The West Indian negro sometimes adores his Voodoo Snake.

A small and strident section of Englishmen has always adored Communist Russia.

All three cults were equally unreasonable, and no doubt it was an equal waste of time to try to reason with the devotees of any one of these faiths. The crude truth is that Russia under the Tsars was always held up as the most backward of European countries, but an objective study of Russia under the Soviets shows a general decline in civilization from that of Russia under the Tsars.

Both systems have maintained in turn a secret police accountable to nobody but its chief for its actions. Both have imprisoned, condemned and executed without trial for so-called political offences. The one has persecuted the Jews, the other Christians. But while the Tsars towards the end at least permitted the existence of a Free Parliament in which Democrats, Liberals and even Socialists were allowed to express their views, the spectacle of Monarchist deputies stating their opinions in an elected assembly under the Soviets would always have been utterly unthinkable.

Men, Martyrs and Mountebanks

In the last twenty years of Tsarist tyranny, Russia produced much that was beautiful and some things that were great. Tolstoy, Tchekov, Dostoevsky, Scriabin, Nijinski, Chaliapine, Pavlova and Leon Bakst belong to those decades. But twenty years of Bolshevist tyranny produced one or two competent film directors, and that is all.

It was often argued that Bolshevism improved the workers' standard of living. Its admirers apparently accepted this as a complete justification for deliberately exterminating three million members of the middle class. There has been an improvement. Considering the advances made all over the world, it would have been remarkable if there had been none.

In Russia 90 per cent of the people are peasants, and out of those peasants 20 per cent used to own a cow under the Tsars. Under the Communists the proportion had fallen to 4 per cent. On the other hand, the champions of Soviet Government argued that the peasants were 'happier' in collective farms. They had better be. Those who showed they felt otherwise have simply been branded as Kolaks, uprooted from their holdings, and sent to die in the frozen North. This process, known as liquidation, extended to several millions. One whole people, the Kuban Cossacks, appears to have vanished completely. Executions and mass shootings have never stopped, and it is a poor advertisement for the success of any system when twenty years after its institution the rulers still found it necessary to execute most of the prominent officers in their army.

In the industrial field, the achievements of the Soviets are said to be considerable. We were always

Stalin Plays His Hand

hearing of their new factories. We never seemed to see anything that was made in them but we were always hearing how wonderful they were.

Personally conducted tours with Government-appointed guides showed foreign visitors new car plants, dams and model prisons. At least they showed them a new car plant, a dam and a model prison. The Dam—it is at Dniepostroi—was one of the greatest Soviet achievements. We grew tired of hearing about it. Built by American engineers because Russia had murdered her own, it was the largest Dam in Europe; and it fed the most powerful hydro-electric plant in the world with a maximum capacity of a million horsepower.

But whether this vast reserve of power was ever, in fact, generated, and what factories it served and what they produced in them, was quite impossible ever to discover. The Dam at Dniepostroi was the culminatory achievement of the Russian Five Year plan started in 1927, that vast project which was designed to furnish the country with the means to supply all her industrial needs by 1932. When it started we were told that Russia would swamp the world in 1933 with the products of her vast new plant. We were assured that Russian goods could be so cheaply produced since there was no need for profits and dividends that no capitalist country would be able to compete with them. But every year that the Five-Year plan went on we seemed to hear less about it. And when the five years were over we heard nothing about it at all. What became of it? I really do not know. Certainly the promised goods did not materialize. But in 1939 the world had ceased to be interested in the Five-Year plan.

Another menace was rising to replace it, and that menace was Adolf Hitler.

There is excellent authority for the theory that you cannot expel devils by the aid of Beelzebub. It goes back 2,000 years at least. But between 1933 and 1939 Englishmen were slow to heed it. There was a school that believed Communist Russia was a check on Nazism, and there was a school that thought Nazi Germany was a barrier to Communism. Both found every encouragement from their respective favourites, and the two Governments went into competition for the friendly opinion of British and American visitors in general and novelists in particular.

The Dam at Dniepostroi was set up against the New Reich's motorways, and as everything was done to make these visits enjoyable, both sides made their converts. But both sides in turn underestimated the shrewdness of free men who had not lost their critical faculties, and by 1935 the Nazi-Soviet tussle had resolved itself for most Englishmen into the problem of which was the lesser evil. Few people had realized yet that they were simply variants of the same evil.

One of those few, however, was Winston Churchill, and no man has expressed the truth more neatly than I heard him put it to a meeting in the Albert Hall. "Nazism and Communism may be as very far asunder as the North and the South Poles," he said. "They could indeed not be further. Yet if you were to wake up at either you would not notice the difference."

All the same, the majority came round to the view that on the whole Russia was not so bad as Germany.

There were various reasons for this. Russia always had been a savage country and we expected to read about the cruelties being perpetrated there. Germany, on the other hand, was supposed to be civilized. Communism professed a belief in various excellent ideals. It claimed to be working for Universal Peace, for the Unity of the peoples, the abolition of poverty. Nazism, on the other hand, was never anything but an internal regimentation of a brave but docile people.

One evening at Chatham House, in London, where there used to be weekly discussions on Foreign Affairs, a visitor put the thoughts of most Englishmen into these words:

"If you ask me whether the standard of living in Germany is higher than the standard of living in Russia . . . it is higher in Germany. But if you ask me if it is higher in Germany to-day than it was in 1934, the answer is it is lower. And if you ask me whether it is higher in Russia to-day than it was in 1914, the answer is it is higher."

Besides, the Russian approach was not at first so crude as the German. Both revolutions were aggressive. Both threatened their neighbours. But while the Nazis used to send their mechanized armies into neighbour countries, the Bolshevik's technique was to burrow from within, to try to stir up revolutions through the local Communist Party.

This remained their policy even when they had apparently disavowed Lenin's Gospel of World Revolution and exiled Trotsky for supporting it. The attack was carried out not by the Government but by the Comintern, the governing body of that world-wide Union of Communist Parties called the Third International. The relationship of the Soviet Government to the Comintern was as hard to define as the relationship of the German Government to the Nazi Party.

This duality went so far that while the Soviet Government, professedly in alliance with France, was urging the French people to stand firm for Czechoslovakia in the autumn of 1938, the French Communist Party were busy at the same time fomenting strikes in the French aeroplane works.

Yet because the Soviet evil was subtle and the Nazi evil was crude, the British Government was at last compelled by the weight of public opinion to open negotiations with Russia in order to form a common plan for the defence of Poland. The negotiations began in March 1939, and they finally broke down in August when Russia reached an agreement with her natural ally Germany.

They broke down and there are many of us who are glad that they did so.

For the price of Russian aid was that we should be accomplices while her loathsome persecutions, her secret police and her liquidating process were extended into the territories of those free democracies that lay on her Western border. As I write, that tragedy is actually coming to pass. Finland is under the hammer. But at least we are not accomplices.

Had we been willing to agree to the Russian terms last spring the situation in Eastern Europe and the position of the Red Army there would probably have been precisely what they are to-day. But there would have been this great difference. The blood of all those Polish landowners, soldiers, policemen and peasants who were so foully hunted to death by the Reds in Eastern Poland, the Communist domination

Stalin Plays His Hand

inflicted on the Baltic republics of Latvia, Esthonia and Lithuania, the sufferings of martyred Finland—all these would have lain on the conscience of the British Government and the British people. For the moment we have been powerless to prevent them, but at least we were not privy to them.

There is this also to consider. Ever since 1918 the existence of that vast prison-house that is Soviet Russia, where freedom was stifled and all the worst instincts of malice, envy and class hatred were constantly kept at their highest pitch in order to make the wheels of government go round, have made it impossible to reach a settlement in Europe along those lines of Freedom, Justice and Contentment that alone could have made Peace enduring. So long as that threat to freedom existed the nations would not disarm. What is true of the past will be true of the future as well. If we had come to the conference table at the end of this war as partners of Communist tyranny, obliged to hear its demands and to consult its wishes, we could never have drawn up the Peace treaty that we dream of, the only Peace that can make the tragedy we are living through worth while.

One evening in 1934 a friend of mine sat down to dinner with the only man who has ever given freedom to Russia. The freedom lasted for six months, and the man's name is Alexander Kerensky. My friend told me how he reflected that this unassuming and undistinguished-looking guest held a greater sway over more people at a more vital moment in their history than any other man that has ever lived. Kerensky failed and he has been harshly and probably justly judged for that failure.

Men, Martyrs and Mountebanks

As the night wore on, my friend began to talk rather frankly, and finally he asked Kerensky outright whether he still had any hopes.

"For myself, do you mean, or for Russian democracy?"

"Don't they amount to roughly the same thing?"

"Not quite," said Kerensky. "I happen to be mortal."

"And Russian democracy?"

"That is undying. I do not believe that any country that has once known freedom will be content to stay permanently a slave."

"Even if it only knew freedom for five months?"

"Even if it only knew it for five days," said Kerensky.

CHAPTER IX

Visitor to Paris

1938—THE YEAR OF ENDLESS CRISES— was drawing to its close. The month of December had arrived, and a world almost at peace was preparing for the Christmas festival.

It was at the beginning of this merry month that a special carriage which had been detached from the Nord Express drew into the quiet little Gare des Invalides, in Paris. The distinguished passenger stepped out. It was Herr von Ribbentrop, Foreign Minister of the German Reich.

With a tactfulness that was by no means Teutonic, he had taken off his uniform (the resplendent black and silver of a Nazi *Reichsaussenminister*) while he was still in the train. Thus it was in a lounge suit that he drove in a fast car with a motor-cycle escort along the *quais*. One or two tourists, purchasing paper-covered books on "*l'amour*", looked up to see the cavalcade go by. Otherwise the route had not been so deserted since the victorious Prussian army marched through Paris in 1871.

When von Ribbentrop reached the Hôtel de la Couronne, he put on his uniform again. The ordeal of the streets was over, and he felt secure.

He had come to sign that epoch-making document that was to be one of history's magnificent moments. Those ancient and inconvenient enemies, France and Germany, had concluded a treaty of enduring friendship for all time. Not for Hitler and Ribbentrop a mere fifty years of peace. The writ of the Fuehrer would run through eternity.

And Ribbentrop had come to Paris to sign the document. Another of those swift, spectacular, and fleeting triumphs which had raised him to such giddy heights. Unfortunately for him he had chosen the worst possible setting for the great reconciliation scene. There are two cities where ridicule kills. One is Dublin, the other is Paris. There is a laughter that slays the victim with the finality of Cock Robin. There is no mirth in such laughter, it is a sharp and cruel sound instead.

Ribbentrop saw himself as the centre of a historical, romantic drama. Paris laughed at him as if he were the demon king in a pantomime. Yet the pale-eyed visitor had found a shrewd and certainly substantial backer for his plot. He came to Paris sponsored by no less a personage than his counterpart, M. Georges Bonnet. Two Foreign Secretaries with a single policy. Two hearts that beat as one. M. Bonnet had power in moneyed circles. Therefore his influence extended to unexpected places. He was the hero or the villain of a hundred whispered stories. Ever since Munich he had been the favourite topic of conversation in the drawing-rooms of Paris. M. Bonnet wanted appeasement with Germany. He wanted it at almost any price. As a man of great influence and a Minister of Foreign Affairs he was in a position to assist the achievement of his desires. For one thing, the President of the Council, M. Edouard Daladier, was not sure of himself. It is always the opportunity of the second man when his chief is bewildered by alternatives.

Visitor to Paris

It is difficult to realize the delicacy of M. Daladier's position towards the end of 1938.

Only a few months before he had taken over from the well-meaning but incompetent Popular Front Government of M. Blum. As an inheritance it had proved full of embarrassments. There was also the memory of four years back, when the Staviski riots had occurred. M. Daladier was in power, and it was he who was held responsible for firing into a crowd that was marching on the Chamber of Deputies from the Place de la Concorde. His friends said that he had never lost the look of horror that appeared in his fine blue eyes that day.

Truly, M. Daladier could ask if ever a leader was so beset with enemies. The mob that he had fired on were of the Right Wing—so he could not count on sympathy from the Conservatives.

The Government that he had ousted was of the Left—and he could hardly look for support from the Socialists. Therefore, in the first month of his 1938 Government, he had had to balance himself precariously on such groups as were content to bear his weight. M. Bonnet was pleased. Secure of his fortune and of his connections, he pursued the path of appeasement, convinced that he would have his way.

So there had come Munich. M. Bonnet saw his first dreams come true. M. Daladier, flying home from Munich, circled the aerodrome over and over again because he thought the French people below had come to curse him.

From Munich to the December visit of Ribbentrop was a logical step in M. Bonnet's scheme. The preparations were behind the scenes, but the whole plan eventually came into the open, and so a special car was added to the Nord Express. Herr von Ribbentrop works quickly, his departures are swifter than his arrivals. Therefore in the afternoon M. Bonnet collected his reward—the "no more war" pact between Germany and France, enemies for a thousand years, had put the seal of success upon his long endeavours. But in the evening there was a reception, held in honour of the distinguished German Minister. One guest, however, did not turn up. His name was M. Georges Mandel, Minister of the Colonies. Normally his absence would not have been extraordinary, since M. Mandel happens to be a Jew. But actually it signified something far more than mere pride of race. When M. Mandel refused to attend the reception that night he did so as a Frenchman convinced that he was interpreting the spirit of his own country.

Once he was known as Jeroboam Rothschild, and was "Tiger" Clemenceau's right-hand man in the hour of victory. Thus he represented the old school of French patriots, the glory of yesterday as opposed to the murky greyness of the transitory hour. As a man he was never popular. He was probably the best Postmaster-General France ever had. He was certainly the best hated. Yet on that evening when he stayed away from the Ribbentrop reception, the Jew who had changed his name from Rothschild to Mandel was experiencing an actual popularity.

This tough old political survivor had been waiting his time. He understood the reaction of the French people to Munich better than any other man. He knew that the French were glad that there had been no war. He knew that they hoped for peace. But he also knew that they did not believe in their hearts that peace was possible, and that they felt a bitter shame at their desertion of Czechoslovakia.

Despite the crowds that cheered the arrival of M. Daladier from Munich, the real feeling was one of doubt and shame. As the year progressed, and autumn turned to winter, that dual feeling grew stronger.

Georges Mandel had his ear to the ground, and heard it. M. Bonnet's head was right up in the air, and all he could hear was the singing in his ears caused by the high altitude.

The French Press, in many ways the best informed, but the least informing of its kind, did not give a clear lead. There were *Journaux d'Information*, which only published news, and *Journaux d'Opinion*, which only published comment, principally political, invariably passionate, and usually about each other. There were brilliant journalists in Paris. M. Geraud (Pertinax), and M. Jules Sauerwein have almost no equals in any other country in their infinite knowledge of foreign affairs. But with the exception of two or three Parisian *Journaux d'Information*, the rest of the Paris newspapers are so busy exploiting a certain point of view that it is not easy for the public to gain a complete and coherent picture.

No one visiting Paris in the last two or three years could tell what the French people were thinking merely by reading the newspapers.

And perhaps the French themselves could not have explained their thoughts. There had been so many discouragements. There had been the Communist influence with fewer hours of work, higher wages, disappearing profits, dwindling markets, and chaos of management. There had been scandals which poisoned the wells of public honour. The franc had declined, and truly it seemed that France had entered the twilight which sometimes comes to a great nation when it is too tired to face the challenge of the Fates.

But one man at least kept his faith. It was the old Jew, Georges Mandel. With all the glamour of his association with Georges Clemenceau he urged a policy of strength upon Pierre Daladier. He told him that the French people would rise to any destiny providing there was a leader to guide them. He urged Daladier to be the master of France. By every argument and innuendo he ridiculed, criticized, and condemned the long-nosed Bonnet. "You cannot trust the Communists," he said, "any more than you can trust Bonnet. And I warn you that you cannot trust Flandin, either, with his Right Wing crowd. Flandin was once Prime Minister of France, and he wants to be Prime Minister again."

M. Daladier had never doubted France. He had only doubted himself. With magnificent courage and with a purpose which nothing could crush, he asked only that the flesh should be strong enough to bear his willing spirit. Never in the history of any democracy has a Prime Minister grasped the nettle with greater firmness. The forty-hour week was abolished. An abortive general strike was put down without bloodshed. In finance he had the co-operation of that remarkable man, M. Reynaud. It was M. Reynaud who had called for a pro-League policy and sanctions against Italy when France was determined to keep out of the Abyssinian dispute. France had not forgotten. They said, "This is a man of character who does not

Visitor to Paris

sway with the wind." Backed by M. Daladier, he saved and restored French credit. With M. Mandel to advise him and M. Reynaud to help him, Daladier grew stronger every day. Every day he grew stronger, exerting upon his people an almost Puritanical austerity of conduct, but coupled with a warmth of heart which bound the people to him.

It was in the midst of this very process that M. Bonnet with his head in the air, and Herr von Ribbentrop, with his eye on the future, scratched out their signatures on the short-lived peace treaty. Paris laughed. France echoed that laughter. Those were the signs that M. Daladier had built a healthy body politic to house the sane mind of the French nation. But Ribbentrop, the blunderer, was not content. He asked as a corollary to the agreement that the whole of the French Press should be drilled into approval, or, at any rate, an acquiescence of the Bonnet policy of pro-Nazism. A decree for the control of the Press was actually drawn up and submitted for the signature of the Minister of Justice, M. Marchandeau, who bluntly refused to sign it.

That was the beginning of the end.

There can be no doubt that M. Bonnet acted throughout believing that he was doing so in the best interests of France. One must remember that M. Caillaux, branded as a traitor in 1914, is a citizen of high honour to-day. But the French could not forgive the insolent suggestion that the newspapers of France should be enslaved to the policy of Hitlerism.

And suddenly there was born a phrase.

"*Il faut en finir.*"

It was the Frenchman's equivalent for "We must

get rid of this." Men shrugged their shoulders and said it to each other. Women in the park exchanged it as if it was a greeting. Wave after wave of unhappy refugees—Jews, Democrats, Catholics—German, Austrian, and Czech had broken over the frontiers of France, hunted, hopeless, casting themselves on the humanity and charity of an overburdened France.

"*Il faut en finir.*"

The memory of France went back to those Saturday afternoons when Hitler had staged his famous matinees. There had been mobilizations and semi-mobilizations without number. Business had been paralysed, plans held up, careers disturbed—all because of this Nazi Germany. Even more than that this thing had become a scourge upon the mind. No longer could a Frenchman think or talk of the things closest to his heart. His mind was in the grip of the world obsession with Nazism, and he said, "*Il faut en finir.*"

The storekeeper said it to the housewife who came to market, her basket on her arm, the *concièrge* who keeps the keys said it when he came with the morning paper. It passed into the ears of the motoring tourist from the garage hand who refuelled his car. Like the whisper that ran through the *faubourgs* in the months before the French Revolution, it inflamed the minds of France like a torch.

Then came the march of the Germans into Prague. No longer was it a whisper. It rose louder and louder, as if on an angry wind.

"*IL FAUT EN FINIR.*"

The spring passed, the summer came. Crying that his patience was exhausted, Hitler hurled his troops against the Poles.

Visitor to Paris

Quietly, without flowers or bands, without hysteria or even hatred, France mobilized for war. There were aching hearts, but no tears. The spirit of Daladier and the spirit of Georges Mandel had entered the hearts of France. The silence was more menacing than the frenzy of a mob.

Regiment by regiment, division by division, corps by corps, the citizens of France marched to their place in the Maginot Line.

"*Il faut en finir.*"

But there were other things that were finished, as well. M. Daladier took away M. Bonnet from the Foreign Office, and left him to ruminate upon appeasement in the office of the Ministry of Justice. To show his impartiality, M. Daladier disbanded the Communist movement.

France had found her leader.

Chapter X

The Junior Partner

IT WAS THE BEGINNING OF SUMMER IN THE year of grace 1939, the season when tourists used to come to Italy from Britain, and, better still, from America, and spend their money. Now they would not come. The Axis had ended all that.

Italy was bored.

She missed the elegant, disreputable cosmopolitan just as she missed the gullible traveller. Beads could no longer be sold at an excellent price. In fact, beads could no longer be sold at any price at all. And no one was there to see glass blown into fantastic shapes.

Lace, already obsolescent, was being followed by velvet into cold storage from shop windows. In Venice the pigeons gathered as usual in the Piazza of St. Mark. But there were no shoulders on which to alight, and no Kodaks to immortalize them. The poor, the singers, and the learned had disappeared with the rich, the elegant, and the temptable. A rhythm had been lost, and Italy was bored.

The thrill and daring of Abyssinia had gone, but the uniforms still remained. The Italians, apart from their magnificent northern regiments, are not natural soldiers. Their attitude is the same as that of Disraeli, who said: "A soldier's life is only fit for a fool in peace-time, and a barbarian in war-time."

The Spaniard is a fighter, even a killer. There is no cause for which he will not slay or be slain. The

The Junior Partner

Italian is a trader and an artist. To the merchandise of his genius—architecture, painting, sculpture, glass, velvet, lace—he has never succeeded in adding political genius in the mass. Perhaps it is because of the skies which are so lovely and which make the schemings of men seem tawdry.

Rome was particularly bored.

The Axis, if not broken, was badly bent. Everyone was so weary of the Germans with their uniforms and their lack of money. And what did the Romans care about Danzig? It was bad enough to have to acquire an interest in Addis Ababa, in Libya and in Spain. But why Danzig?

Signor Mussolini was tired. Lacking the megalomania of the perfect dictator, he saw the accomplishments of his régime, great as they were, in true perspective. He had served Italy well. In his own way he had served civilization well, but it had ended wrongly. He was junior partner to a madman in Berchtesgaden. No wonder the high spirits and humour that characterized the Palazza Venezia in early days had been replaced by a grim, uninspiring silence.

His own Party was split into factions. There was Starace, the sea-green little incorruptible, who hated Society, who was austere and small minded, and as ambitious as Fouché. He had such a grip upon the Party as its secretary that one might well wonder if his ambitions did not soar higher still. And Starace was so inartistically pro-German. Everything which had been handed out for foreign consumption about the Axis had found its billet in the receptive brain of the Party secretary. He was for marching wherever

Germany marched, for linking the Mediterranean to the Baltic by a bridge of steel from Rome through Berlin.

Then there was Ciano. A troublesome fellow as a son-in-law. Vital, attractive, clever, but not great. He, too, had succumbed to the arrogance and swashbuckling of the Nazi leaders. It was a pity. It would have been nice to have had a Foreign Minister with a finely detached mind, as befits an Italian statesman. On the opposite side Balbo was making his voice heard from Libya. That is the worst of modern science. Voices carry so easily these days. Balbo was against the anti-Jewish regulations. Balbo was an ardent Catholic, and was speaking in unison with the Vatican.

Then there was Count Grandi, that suave and handsome creature who had kept England's friendship and respect right through the Abyssinian campaign and the fiasco of sanctions. Grandi was against the Axis. He had his own ideas as to Hitler's genius. It was a pity. It is not easy to be a dictator if your hierarchy are divided into opposing camps on questions of such major importance.

Finally, there was the vivacious Alfieri, the Italian counterpart of Dr. Goebbels. A nice fellow, Alfieri, good-looking and gay. Strange that he, too, should be under the influence of Berlin. And finally, of course, there was the Italian people.

Mussolini has never indulged in self-deception. He has always kept his vision clear, his prejudices under control, and his judgment sharpened like a sword. He knew that his prestige with his own people began to decline with the Abyssinian success. It was queer,

The Junior Partner

but it was true. The Italians are easily bored, and tenacity is not one of their qualities. That is why they detest and ridicule the Germans, who hang on to an idea like a dog with a bone.

Compared with the Germans, the Italians regard themselves as men of the world—for does not the whole world come to sunny Italy? They judge the visitors and Western civilization like a connoisseur with his wines. The German tourists, dressed by Baedeker, the women low-heeled, the men loud-voiced, each perspiring with a determination to miss no sight and waste no money, outrage the Italians both physically and aesthetically. The waiter in the Grand Hotel, the urchin in the streets, the merchants and the priests all feel the same distaste. The Roman Empire never conquered Germany. Therefore the German remains a barbarian.

More than that, the Italians fear the Germans, just as a man recognizes the superior strength of the gorilla. The Italian is a philosopher, and realizes that all people are not alike. He knows that warlike nations do exist, like the Turks, the Japanese, and the Germans. A Turk who dies in battle joins Allah, and the Japanese, presumably, have some contract with Paradise—hence the prevalence of suicide. The Italian believes in the next world, but loves this one. He lives with wine, sunshine and women, and loves them all. He sings naturally because music is the voice of happiness. Above all things he detests organization and regimentalism. He wants to sing *la donna è mobile*, and does not give a curse for *Horst Wessel* or any other of the "joy through strength" classics.

Men, Martyrs and Mountebanks

The history of his country is the history of individualism. Men like Garibaldi, Michael Angelo, Cavour, Verdi and Marconi march through the centuries, but they march alone. They do not goose-step in formation. It is charming to see the people play at Fascism. They do it with such zest and good humour. It is like children singing "I am the king of the castle." For the sake of Il Duce, whom they love very much, they try to be serious about it, but they are too charming and individualistic to transform themselves into a forest of eight million bayonets. They are by no means indifferent to the greatness of their past, nor the potentialities of their future. They have their dreams, but they do not intend to share them with the Germans.

Everything that they dislike and fear is typified by the Nazi régime. At the sight of one German they are indifferent. At the sight of two Germans they are bored. At the sight of a hundred Germans they start thinking for themselves, which is against all the rules of totalitarianism.

Therefore Italy was bored as summer came in 1939. Count Ciano decided to go to Bayreuth. It was not that he was fond of music, especially barbarian music, but he wanted to see the senior partner of the firm.

Adolf Hitler was holding court. Everything suited his temperament. On the one hand there was the surging music of Wagner in which he could immerse his soul—that music which has done more to make ordinary men imagine themselves great lovers and great heroes than any other music ever written.

On the other hand there was the Polish crisis coming nearer and nearer to its flash-point.

The Junior Partner

To the super emotionalist like Hitler, it was a perfect setting. Crowds wandering in the streets to try to catch a glimpse of him. His own box at the theatre, where he could appear like a god and drink the elixir of the music of the gods. Messengers arriving from everywhere, visitors from England, drama, melodrama, music, intrigue, power, fear, what more could any vanity-hungry dictator ask?

And to this setting came Count Ciano.

Something went wrong when the two men met. Perhaps Ciano was lacking in mysticism. It was as if Prince Danilo had appeared in the last act of *The Twilight of the Gods*.

"I urge you to go slow," said Ciano. "Danzig is bound to fall into your hands like a ripe pear. Why have a war about it? You know very well that England and France are pledged to Poland. This time they mean business, and if you go ahead nothing can prevent war. As strongly as possible I urge you to consider the full consequences of what you are doing."

Herr Hitler, who was in a high state of exaltation, found the words displeasing. When German generals trembled in his presence, and high Nazi officials prostrated themselves before him, who was this Italian swashbuckler to tell him to hold back the thunderbolts of Jove?

"Do you think Danzig is all I want?" he roared. "It is only the beginning of what I want and what I shall have."

To that extent the scene has become known. What followed is still a matter of rumour and to some extent conjecture, but it appears that somewhere in the performance Hitler made the mistake of snapping his fingers. Maybe he was snapping them at England or France or Colonel Beck. Count Ciano took it that he was snapping them at him. The son-in-law of Mussolini did not attempt to hide his anger.

When he left Bayreuth his brow was covered with frowns, nor had they disappeared when he reached Italy. For several nights he dined alone in public, and no one saw him smile. A close friend at last invaded his reticence.

"How did you find Hitler?" he asked.

Ciano's jaw stiffened.

"The fellow is mad," he answered.

Then an interesting thing happened. At a bathing place near Rome Ciano and some of his friends in the Foreign Office were enjoying the sun. The war had already begun, and Poland was meeting alone the full impact of the German forces.

The Polish Ambassador to Rome walked by. With the impetuous warmth of their race, Ciano and his colleagues at once went over to him and overwhelmed him with friendly and sympathetic greetings. Only one of the group stood aside. A friend of mine who was there asked the one recalcitrant Foreign Office official why he had not followed the others.

"I could not face the Polish Ambassador," he said. "I felt too great a sense of shame that we have been unable to do anything for them."

Mussolini declared his neutrality. It was said that when the Italian–German alliance had been signed there was a secret clause that it would not be valid if Germany went to war within three years. Rumour had it that it was under this clause that Mussolini based his neutrality.

The Junior Partner

To my mind the truth goes deeper than that.

I was in Rome when Chamberlain went there. I saw the Italian people in the streets holding out their hands towards Chamberlain as if he had come from another world to save them from the darkness which was oppressing them. I saw women weep. On that visit the heart of Italy spoke as clearly as a voice from a mountain top. Mussolini heard that voice, and did not try to check it. There were still harsh memories of Abyssinia and the futile days of sanctions, but there were also memories that went back for a thousand years, when Britain had always been the friend of Italy, and never the oppressor.

I came away from that visit convinced that no one, not even Mussolini, could bring the Italian people into war against us, and, what is more, I felt that Mussolini had no intention of trying it. Even when the alliance was signed between Germany and Italy I founded my faith on the atmosphere of that significant visit in January 1939.

There were those, of course, who made good jokes about Italy's neutrality. There were amateur strategists and Pall Mall wits who said that we should force Italy to fight against us so as to draw the German forces to her relief. Such jokes were worthy of those who made them. The fact is that the Mediterranean has remained, so far, a friendly lake.

A few months before the war there were many who feared that Italy and Spain would come in with Germany. Nor did their fears end there. They foresaw the Pacific dominated by the Japanese with outrages, if not actual war, against our isolated nationals in the Far East. They visualized the Spanish army menacing France, with Spanish ports as bases for German U-boats. They saw our Mediterranean lifeline cut by the Italian surface fleet and submarines.

It was the same picture, but with different feelings that Hitler saw as he listened to the mesmeric music of his favourite master.

But the outbreak of hostilities brought strange developments.

Mussolini had said: "We shall take no military initiative."

In Spain General Franco sent for Marshal Pétain, the French Ambassador.

It was a historic moment in the destiny of the world, and I give it as told to me by the Duke of Alba, Franco's Ambassador to London.

It had been a stroke of genius to send the great French marshal as a plenipotentiary to Spain when the civil war had ended. General Franco is a soldier, and he respected the great soldier from France who had been his tutor at the military academy. Where the most adroit diplomat might have failed, the marshal succeeded.

"I have a message for your government," said General Franco, "and I would be grateful if Your Excellency would transmit it to them. I wish you to assure M. Daladier and his ministers, on my word of honour, that France need not keep one soldier on the Pyrenees frontier."

The marshal thanked him with a warmth which needs no underlining. As swiftly as possible he sent the message to Paris. The reply was worthy of Daladier. It was to the effect that he accepted the assurances of General Franco without equivocation, and that the

The Junior Partner

French troops stationed at the frontier would be moved at once to where they could become part of the battle formation against Germany.

But to return to Italy.

She was no longer bored. Certainly there were exasperations about a war of blockade, and there was a strain which no nation in Europe could escape. But at last the nightmare of the Axis had disappeared. True, it was not officially broken or denounced. It was still there, suspended like the sword of Damocles, but it was a sword with a blunted edge. Italian luxury liners openly sailed the seas, and did good business, for no one feared that a German submarine would sink them. Italian traders set out for markets now blocked to Germany. The instinct of the Neapolitan to buy and sell was finding free expression once more.

At regular intervals in the day and night Rome began to broadcast in English. From the very first it was unbiased and dignified. With the utmost courtesy the announcer in English, with his charming Continentalism of speech, would thank us for listening to him, and ask us for suggestions and criticisms. As indirect propaganda it was most effective, since it made you feel that in Rome a gentleman was speaking to you.

Yet there were those in Italy who had not given up the dream of the Axis. Signor Starace did not change his mind. His soul was still crying: "Tunis, Corsica and Nice." He wanted them like a child crying for the light, and he wanted to get them by marching beside the legions of Germany.

The debonair Alfieri was still true to Berlin. In

spite of Italian neutrality the newspapers of Rome would unexpectedly deliver a violent attack upon the democracies. It was not sustained, as of old, but, brief as it was, it would puzzle those who believed that we were looking on a new Italy.

Two months went by. On the last day of October, M. Molotov was to make an earth-shattering announcement in Moscow. The Germans had heralded it with such a beating of drums and roaring of threats that the whole world poised itself ready to receive the shock.

Hitler must have had the most precise assurances as to the contents of the speech or he would not have expended so much breath in calling upon the world to listen.

But on the morning of the last day in October Rome spoke first. It was to announce a readjustment of the principal offices of State.

Signor Starace was no longer to be Secretary of the Party. Instead, he was to take charge of the Fascist militia, including the little boys of seven and eight belonging to the Ballila. Signor Alfieri was asked to surrender his baton of propaganda. With great consideration he had been promoted to the post of Ambassador Expectant. Later, he was appointed Ambassador to the Vatican, which enabled him to get home every night from his work.

Berlin rushed to the microphone:

"It is absurd for Great Britain to pretend that these changes are of the slightest political significance. It is the custom of the Italian Government from time to time to readjust its Cabinet for purposes of efficiency. The present changes in no way alter the basic policy

The Junior Partner

of the Italian nation. Italy and Germany understand one another completely."

In Britain we nodded our heads approvingly. Germany and Italy understood one another completely.

We could ask for no more.

Chapter XI

Polonaise Militaire

THE IMMEDIATE OCCASION OF HOSTILITIES was Germany's invasion of Poland. It happened without any declaration of war on September 1st, 1939.

But the Polish problem did not cause the war. That cannot be over-emphasized. By the time the Nazis turned on their Eastern neighbours, British opinion knew that the next time Hitler committed an act of aggression Britain would have to fight. That his next act happened to be directed against the Poles was, to most Englishmen, merely by the way.

Yet Britain would have done well to consider Poland a little more closely ; to realize just what she had meant in the history of Western civilization.

Count Raczynski, the Polish Ambassador in London, said "Poland is always in the front line." For six hundred years she stood with Hungary on the Eastern Marches of Europe. While her armoured warriors held off the successive waves of Turks and Tartars we were able to build much that we call Western civilization behind the rampart of their bodies. In the years that followed the war of 1914, she stood between Bolshevism and the West. It was the Polish legionaries who held the tide of the Red Revolution from the walls of Warsaw in 1921, and rolled it back again to those Eastern Marches from which it flowed.

Always in the front line, Poland was once more

Polonaise Militaire

called upon in 1939 to give her manhood for civilization in that vital breathing space when France and Britain moved to their war positions. Three times she has saved the West. Herself she could not save. High up on the sandstone spire of the cathedral at Cracow, where Poland's kings lie buried, the hour is sometimes sounded by a silver trumpet. And at the fifth note of eight the trumpet falters, its notes suddenly broken in memory of the day when the trumpeter fell transfixed by a Tartar arrow as he stood there sounding the hour.

That broken call is the story of Poland. She has given great names to enrich the heritage she fought so bravely to preserve. Chopin, Paderewski, Madame Curie, Joseph Conrad. . . . It was her tragedy that all these have made their careers outside their country. For in 1794 Poland was obliterated from the map of Europe, and her land was divided among the three Empires on her border, three Empires from whose wreckage she arose in 1919, a nation once again.

She was plunged into nationhood, but without the technique of government to call upon. She had no trained civil service. For it was only in the Austrian provinces that Poles were allowed to enter the civil service. She had no middle class. The jealousy of her conquerors had seen to it that her commerce should never be in Polish hands. For 150 years her territory had been stripped bare to glut the Prussians and Russians. In the World War she was ravaged by their armies as they struggled for possession of her soil. Against this background Poland blundered into the sunlight of her nationhood.

Her new birth came at a time of pestilence and famine. Every conceivable difficulty beset the men who re-founded their country. Be it admitted they made grave mistakes. Fierce patriotism and a long memory had served to keep alive the flame of Polish nationalism in the years when there was no Poland outside the hearts and the dreams of her people. In those dark years the Polish ideal endured so stubbornly that there never was a time when the last fight for freedom lay beyond the memory of men and women still alive. But memory, idealism, and resentment are not always the best foundations for nationhood.

As in the days of servitude Poland continued to dwell in her ancient past. "These Germans," said a Polish general to Walter Duranty, the *New York Times* correspondent, in the July of 1939, "will be useless. We shall beat them as we did at Tannenberg."

"At Tannenberg?" said Duranty, surprised as he remembered Hindenburg's great victory.

"I mean the real battle of Tannenberg," the Pole explained, "the one we fought in 1400."

Brave, proud, obstinate, the Poles managed to quarrel with all their neighbours at once: with Russia over the Ukraine, with Germany about Silesia, with the Lithuanians because of Vilna, and with the Czechs for the sake of Teschen. Surrounded by enemies on every side, sandwiched between Germany and Russia, rent by their memory of the years when they were enslaved, Poland's rulers feared every alien minority that might weaken their nationhood. This in a country where one-third of the population was an alien minority was unfortunate, to say the least. Perhaps it would have been better to draw other conclusions from the past, to learn from it how little persecution pays. Yet if the Ukrainians, the Germans, and the Jews in Poland often had little reason to hail the resurrection of the young Republic, it should be remembered that fear is at the root of most human misdeeds, and that in the short second life of Poland there was always good reason to be afraid.

It was fear that made Poland replace the visionary Paderewski with Pilsudski, the soldier patriot, and to entrust the direction of the country after he died to a clique of colonels who substituted an unimaginative regimentation for the deeper unity that might have been created. And out of fear they never quite trusted either the industrial masses or the great families, the Potockis, Radziwills, and Lubomirskis, with their due share in the national Government, and so deprived their country of the gifts they might have brought to the task.

Yet in the face of danger Poland was suddenly united as she had never been before. In the summer of 1939 her people stood to arms without distinction of race or class; noble and peasant, Pole, Ukrainian and Jew.

The command was less skilful than the men were brave. In strategy as in politics, their minds still lived in the past, in the days when the Polish cavalry were wont to boast that if the heavens fell they would catch them on their lances. Proud, brave, obstinate, they would not hear about fortified lines and the strategy of retreat. "We rely on our mobility," they said. "The mechanized army that invades us will flounder in our mud, and then! Our cavalry will cut them down like grass."

On this proud, brave people the Nazis fell with the full mechanized might they had been preparing for five years. Outnumbered, outranged, outmanœuvred, and overwhelmed, the various units of the Polish army lost contact with their leaders and with each other. Great flights of German bombers made an inferno of their communications, while chains of fighter planes swooped mercilessly down with machine guns on the Polish cavalry. Against terrific odds the Polish airmen battled frantically when they could get their machines up into the air. As the Germans had destroyed half their aerodromes, this was not very often. With the dash of their ancient riders, the pilots charged the enemy planes, bringing them down in their glorious suicide rather than use their parachutes or land.

With rifle and bayonet the infantry stood in the way of Germany's advancing tanks, and in the hopeless battle they inflicted heavy losses on the Germans, far heavier than Hitler had reckoned or dared to admit. With that savage ferocity which they always employ against small nations, the Germans pursued the grim war of extermination to its cruel end. From north, south and west they rolled relentlessly over the fields of Poland. Even so, in the Eastern Marches the Poles might yet have re-formed and held their enemy indefinitely at bay. But at the beginning of the third week of war the Russian army began its westward march, plunging its deadly thrust into the back of the Polish forces. There has been nothing in history more cynical. The Reds had avenged their defeat of 1921, and Poland, beset from all sides, could resist no longer.

As in all national tragedies the fate of the leaders was varied and dramatic. The astutest of the clique of colonels, Beck, of the neat dress and superb address, the cleverest politician, perhaps, in Europe, vanished from the scene, and no newspaper bothered

Polonaise Militaire

to enquire what had happened to him. Marshal Smigly-Rydz, the Prime Minister, Pilsudski's successor, bundled President Moscicki across the Rumanian border, where they both arrived in safety.

Prince Radziwill, the old Conservative leader, refused to leave the house that had belonged to so many generations of his ancestors, and waited there till death and the Russians found him. Bernard Mond, Poland's only Jewish general, died leading a last bayonet charge.

Yet the true hero of the Polish war was not a soldier. He was M. Stefan Starzynski, the Mayor of Warsaw. Abandoned by his President and his Prime Minister, beset on all sides by his enemies, betrayed by his neutral neighbour, and with no hope of aid from his allies in the West, he organized the last defences of the capital. And then, when all else was lost, with the roar of the enemy planes perpetually over their heads, with their homes tumbling about them in ruins as the great Krupp siege guns ploughed mercilessly away, the people of the Polish capital fought on for their city. It was a magnificent stand. For two weeks they fought that fight which could have only one ending. Just as 150 years before them Kosciuszko peasant bands struggled with scythes against the Russian and the Prussian cannon, so did these men battle on with their rifles behind tramcar and paving-stone barricades against the tanks and bombers that came ceaselessly against them.

Again and again the great caterpillar-wheels rolled into action till it seemed there could be no breath left where they had passed. Again and again the flickers of resistance spluttered into another burst of life. Fainter and fainter it grew as the corpses were piled high, till the silence spread itself over the ruins, and there was nothing but a great emptiness to greet the victor.

So Poland died once more. And in the heroism of her death she was again reborn. Once again she had held her head in pride against the Barbarians. Only this time they came from the West. She was the first to say "No" to Hitler. He will not forget that. She paid a heavy price, as Hitler has never ceased to remind Europe. But history will not forget, either.

The Austrian army say they would have resisted the Nazi tide, save that no orders came. The Czechs protest that they were betrayed by their allies. But the Poles did stand, and because of that they have imposed on all who value freedom the solemn duty to see that Poland lives again.

Perhaps it will be a better nation that comes out of the fire. It could not be a braver.

Chapter XII

Black-out

ON FRIDAY, AUGUST 30TH, TWO DAYS BEFORE war, London saw its first black-out. It was a cloudy night and there was a slight drizzle. Only a few thin crosses on the traffic lights and the screened side lamps of motor-cars penetrated, here and there, the wall of stifling darkness with a feeble watery gleam. The effect on a London whose eyes were attuned to powerful arc lamps and neon lighting was that of a suddenly darkened room. We were bemused, lost utterly. People bumped through the black-out into lamp posts and stumbled off kerbs. Drivers with screaming brakes skidded to avoid pedestrians sighted when it was too late. The hospitals began to receive their first wartime casualties and they were not the victims of enemy action.

That week-end the great evacuation began. They emptied the hospitals. Every London infirmary was cleared of its patients and all the metropolitan doctors were dumped at their new posts up and down the land leaving their old patients to get well as best they could without them. The schools were evacuated; all of them. Those parents, and they were the majority, who objected to their children being carted away were left with no school to send them to since the teachers were swept off along with their pupils. In the morning they assembled complete with their gas masks at the school. In the afternoon there trooped down the high streets of sundry country towns droves of bemused school children all labelled and numbered like unwilling exhibits and preceded by placards announcing which school they came from. At the tail of the pitiful procession toddled the five- and six-year-olds, one hand tightly clasping that of an older girl, the other screwed into eyes red from weeping. Flustered mistresses received them at village schools where they ran through long lists of likely billets and they duly appeared in their twos and threes at the doors of houses and cottages more or less prepared for them.

The evacuation went off with Andersonian precision. The reception was not quite so happy. Sir John Anderson's favourite poet once wrote "that East is East and West is West and never the twain shall meet". And a meeting of extremes is not brought about by enforced juxtaposition. The East End children thrust into Essex manor houses revealed a world that was inexplicable to a world that they found incomprehensible.

A conspiracy of patriotic silence could not conceal the shock that followed this wholesale invasion of the Englishman's home by droves of unfamiliar children not always either mannerly or spotless. Nothing could hide the utter bewilderment of the little transplanted beings torn out of their homes and thrust unoccupied upon a strange and startled world.

There were many that day who were first shocked then horrified and then ashamed to see those poor grimy grubbly little things who were suddenly planted in their homes. Yet there were many who rose above instinct and emotion to take them not to their homes only but to their hearts also.

Black-out

It has been said 'Suffer little children to come unto Me' and the full story of their coming to the English countryside will never be told. Yet there were many homes in England and some of them were very stately indeed, that were livelier and happier that day for the arrival of these unexpected guests. There were many mansion houses set in fair lawns and terraces but set above all in silence and in loneliness—that grim loneliness of the English countryside which is vaster than that of the prairies. Under the new social revaluation they were happier and warmer for the laughter of the children. And there were noble houses in the English shires that dreaded the day they were to leave as much as ever they had feared the day of their coming.

In town and country, throughout the length and breadth of Britain, it was a sudden and violent revolution.

In places it may be that it was unnecessarily violent. Had empty houses been commandeered for schools with the zeal with which they were commandeered for the Civil Service there would have been less shattering of that privacy of home life which is, to the Englishman, the essence of his very existence. Had the children been boarded together with their teachers in buildings specially taken over there would have been less resentment among the young evacuees. As it was, they too often acquired at the most sensitive period of their lives, a bitterness against the world which seemed so inexplicably and so unreasonably different.

Government departments were evacuated too ; at least they evacuated a considerable proportion of them.

Men, Martyrs and Mountebanks

It has been said that His Majesty's Government is, in the last resort, a Civil Service clerk earning £600 a year. The British Civil Servant is zealous, hard-working and of an integrity that has no parallel. He is apt, however, to be over precise, intolerant and above all unimaginative. Pursuing a regular round, secure in a regular salary, his life arranged along the bus routes between Whitehall and the South-Western suburbs, the £600 a year clerk suddenly found himself vested with the power to move Birnam Wood to Dunsinane with a few taps on the typewriter. He often acquired a sudden Napoleon complex. An invading army could hardly have been more high-handed or less considerate than these Government clerks when they started commandeering hotels, schools, institutions, country houses and everything else that took their fancy, at forty-eight hours' notice without compensation or consideration for the inmates. Meddling degenerated into muddling.

Ancient Public Schools were suddenly uprooted and left to shift for themselves. One was shunted to the dangerous neighbourhood of an arms factory so that the Civil Servants apparently might enjoy the safety and sea air of the Welsh coast. A big hotel in a West Country Spa was taken over without a moment's thought for the guests, many of whom were invalids who had made their homes there for twenty-five years. Hotels, in fact, were commandeered wholesale, the staffs were thrown out of work, the proprietors lost their incomes, their livelihoods, their capital and their homes.

"Our school," wrote one head mistress, "was subjected to hustle of the most ruthless character, leaving

Black-out

laboratories, art rooms, and chapel to be used for clerks, valuable scientific instruments were flung from first-floor windows, many things were lost or stolen, and quantities damaged or ruined by unskilled handling." And all this "in a secrecy such that it was impossible to make any effective provisional arrangement to avoid the confusion that was bound to result."

Perhaps the story lacks nothing for the writer's indignation.

Assailed by people, Parliament and Press, exposed overnight to the remorseless glare of an entirely unaccustomed publicity, the Civil Servants at any rate worked through those nights and days as they had never worked before. Behind the shutters of what was left of Whitehall and in all their improvised offices set up in sundry unexpected places there was no blackout during 24 hours out of the 24.

In London, from the moment when war was declared on the Sunday, the transformation of the front doorstep to the front line was in appearance complete.

The streets contained one quarter of their usual population, and half that quarter wore shrapnel helmets and service respirators. Everybody was standing by an ambulance or standing by a hospital, or just standing by.

Nobody ventured out even to post a letter without his gas mask. People who had read the details of the bombing of Guernica and Shanghai, and seen a dozen films that depicted the obliteration of cities from the air had been keyed up in the past twelve hours by two (false) alarms from a siren whose very note seemed designed to terrify, as I have described it. It was no wonder if they expected Western civilization to end before lunch-time.

London was no longer a metropolis, no longer a living, pulsating thing. Nothing was missing, nothing marked. But London had become a tomb—a memory of far-off days when her heart-beat was like an anvil stroke.

It is the boast of every Englishman that his house is his castle. Now he could go further than that. His house was his prison.

Those of us who lived there were prisoners on parole. We were allowed out during the day, but on our word of honour to return before dusk and incarcerate ourselves hermetically in our cells for the night.

Not a theatre was open in the West End. The unhappy cinemas in the centre of London after a period of complete obliteration were allowed to open until 6 p.m. Few people went to them. The public had enough darkness without buying it in the daytime.

Twice I dined next door, and on three reckless occasions I went to the Savoy or some place to dine with friends. We carried our gas masks to the table, and at eleven o'clock or so began the crawl home in the pitch blackness. Not a ray of light came from any house. Even if the door was opened the black curtains kept the interior shrouded.

Ironically, for there was irony in everything those days, the sun shone incessantly. We had four weeks of heavenly weather.

Let us walk through the Park to Westminster.

For a moment the pulses quicken at the thought. The Park in early autumn sunshine! Perhaps life has

Black-out

not lost its sparkle, after all. But there is something missing. One's eyes stray curiously from side to side. What are they looking for? What familiar feature has gone?

Then it comes upon you. There are no children. The parade of the nannies with their perambulators, the running youngsters and jumping dogs, they have vanished as completely as if a Pied Piper had enticed them to some never-never land. London is a city without children.

At Parliament Square you pause unconsciously for the swirl of the traffic that normally keeps you at bay until a polite constable holds up the torrent to allow the elected legislator to reach the Houses of Parliament.

The torrent has become a placid stream. Two or three cars, perhaps, and you can stroll across without risk to life or limb. No traffic, no children, no dogs, no lights, no cinemas, no theatres.

And the raiders did not come.

Apparently clear of that menace for the moment, Londoners began to look round and to take stock. London was flooded with beams of a harvest moon that discovered strange beauties, hitherto unsuspected, even though all the contrivances of flood lighting had been brought into play to discover them in the past.

Londoners noticed other things besides moonlit buildings. They began to be slightly self-conscious.

They had been reminded with some frequency of the way that their forefathers had faced danger when Queen Bess was at Tilbury or Napoleon's army at Boulogne, and some of them wondered what Drake and Nelson would have thought about evacuating the Admiralty.

Men, Martyrs and Mountebanks

A girl driver at a West End London A.R.P. station ventured to say that some people might regret having been absent in those first critical days. "Madam, that may be twaddle, but it's Shakespeare," said an auxiliary fireman, whose mind recalled a certain speech put into Henry V's mouth on the eve of Agincourt.

Because Sir John Anderson had laid a solemn bar on all gatherings of more than thirty people, lectures, schools, concert rooms, dance halls, cinemas, and theatres were closed, while public houses remained open, an arrangement hardly calculated to improve our sobriety. Lord Hugh Cecil wrote a letter to *The Times* suggesting that the advisability or otherwise of risking his life was a thing the individual should decide for himself. One week's black-out caused five hundred deaths without a bomb being dropped. Businesses that had transferred to the depths of forests and the slopes of mountains suddenly awoke to the fact that there were no customers. Other businesses that had remained in London lay marooned in a desert denuded of colleagues and clients.

The Bank of England clerks wandered sheepishly round hutments in the South-West suburbs. The Ministry of Fisheries hurriedly removed to St. John College, Oxford, found that the Isis is not navigable to ocean-going vessels, and Oxford is of all England cities the farthest removed from the sea. Terrific criticism was directed at the British Broadcasting Company, which had scampered still farther West to an address which, although broadcast by the German wireless, was never allowed to be mentioned.

There the staff of Broadcasting House immured

Black-out

itself in an eighteenth-century mansion together with a limited company of music hall artists but an apparently unlimited supply of gramophone records.

From the very first day of the war the B.B.C. was the target for a great deal of deeply felt resentment. Here, it was felt, was one of the greatest movements in the history of the Empire, it may be in the history of all mankind. Never was there such a call for the majesty of great music and the stateliness of English speech. All Britain was there to listen. There was no musician and no actor in all the land who was not ready to hand to give his services, and give them proudly in that great moment of a nation's destiny.

Yet the B.B.C. could do no more than intersperse the grave pronouncements of the statesmen with tinkling trivialities on gramophone discs which were as unfortunate as they were contemptible.

At a time when our first feelings of excited anticipation gave way to an appreciation of the grim struggle ahead of us, and while we were still waiting for those first bombs to fall, the B.B.C. treated us to a talk on "What Happens After Death" (in two parts). A particularly depressing news bulletin about the Polish collapse was followed by the measured cadences of the *Funeral March*. It was not for several moments that a mournful voice above the music told us that a short sketch would follow on the life of Chopin.

The B.B.C. took the criticism manfully, and manfully they withstood it. The programmes drawn up on the basis of intensified air raids and severed communications were hurriedly readjusted, and within three weeks their content was immeasurably improved. Once more there was originality in their ideas, beauty in their music, above all, vitality in their voices. Maybe some prince came through the climbing roses round that West Country retreat to wake the sleeping beauty Broadcasting who lay there. But whatever brought about the sudden transformation scene in British broadcasting in the third week of the war was as much a token as it was a factor in our people's rediscovery of itself.

They were not the only ones whose life was swiftly readjusted by circumstances.

While all business was abruptly brought to a standstill, and large stores were pouring their dismissed employees on to an unresponsive labour market, while bored volunteer firemen came less and less to their posts, and A.R.P. staffs were busy dismissing their paid workers, the first homeward trickle among the evacuees began.

Along with the city schoolchildren a large number of mothers of infants under five had elected to go away into the country. Now, in the absence of any air raid to deter them, 50,000 elected to go back into the towns.

There were many circumstances that decided them. Few had seriously thought over the consequences of their hasty move. The eternal bitterness of what Dante has called "Climbing the staircase of other men," the loneliness of village life where man makes his own pleasures as these city dwellers had never learned to do; the cramped cottage quarters, often without light, water, or drainage; above all, the uninterrupted boredom of having nothing to do were influences not less powerful because few people had enough imagination to foresee them. At the other

Black-out

end of the trail were husbands abandoned and homes broken-up; and grass widowers condemned to lonely houses and meals at eating-houses, when they could find them open.

The Civil Servants might put us into age groups, sex groups, and occupation groups. They might readjust, reassess, and redistribute us between areas styled evacuation, neutral, and reception. But they could neither assess nor redistribute the fundamental emotions and the deep-seated loyalties in the heart and soul of man and woman. They had forgotten that among every section of the community, and most of all, perhaps, among that section that works with its hands, there are certain natural, deep-seated, and enduring instincts that hold a family together. They overlooked or overruled the dependence of a man upon his mate, and the instinctive care that a woman takes of her husband. They forgot what is politely called 'the facts of life.' They forgot also, perhaps, the child's yearning for its parents and for its home. But they could not destroy these things simply by overlooking, overruling, and forgetting them. As the days wore on it became clear, first, that a vast proportion of those scheduled for evacuation had declined to go away, then that many of those who had moved away regretted ever having done so. Only a quarter of Birmingham's 100,000 children scheduled for evacuation were, in fact, evacuated. In Sheffield a mere 6,000 out of 40,000 were moved, and 1,000 of them returned within the month. 60,000 Manchester children out of 92,000 were transported to the surrounding country, but 13,000 swiftly returned again. In Liverpool there were 60,000 who did not go.

Men, Martyrs and Mountebanks

In Sunderland only a third, in Middlesbrough and Leeds a bare quarter took advantage of the scheme.

London was, of all cities, perhaps the most conscious of her danger. But even in London only 270,000 children went into the country out of half a million who should have gone. And out of that number 20,000 returned home again. At times the whole experiment looked likely to collapse.

It was not John Anderson's fault. The machinery of democracy had been called to face problems exceeding the bounds of human experience and human imagination. It was the misfortune of our rulers that at a time when everybody calculated that men's minds would be occupied with the problem of their lives, they were allowed a respite in which to consider the problem of their livings. Poor John Anderson. The enemy air armada might have descended on cities that were shells, whose populations had departed, whose records were removed, and whose treasures were securely stowed away. It might have been that, thanks to him, the chief casualties of the first raid would have occurred among the raiders. Then his countrymen would have said he was the man who did it, and he would have had a statue in Whitehall.

As it was they simply and ungratefully say, "We would rather have had the bombs."

Chapter XIII

The Riddle of the Air

ONE NIGHT AT A PUBLIC MEETING IN LONDON Colonel Moore-Brabazon was speaking. It was in the second year of Hitler's régime, and the famous 'Brab' had drawn a good audience. His sardonic qualities always guaranteed entertainment, and since he was No. 1 Englishman to fly he remains an object of historic interest.

Moore-Brabazon was talking about the development of the aeroplane. Suddenly all humour left him and his face became grimly serious. "When those of us who are called pioneers took up flying," he said, "we did it because we thought that here was something which would bring a great advance in civilization. We believed, in our arrogance, in our foolishness, that our names would be remembered in history as men who had been benefactors to humanity. Now the aeroplane has become a thing of horror. It has become an instrument of death and savagery. Instead of building machines to bring good tidings from one country to another they are built to bring bombs and gas and other devilish things."

Not usually given to dramatic gestures, he brandished his fists towards the ceiling. "We thought our names would be blessed!" he cried. "Instead, we have earned the curse of history."

So spoke the first Englishman to fly.

His sincerity was so evident and his emotion so

deep that it affected us all profoundly. Yet now that we are at war again I wonder if the reverse may not prove true, that the bombing aeroplane may, because of its very horror, finally make war impossible.

At the moment I am writing this, the immense air armada of the Germans is held in its aerodromes. It was loosed with unexampled violence upon the Poles, but since that time has contented itself by sending odd planes or little groups of them to try their luck against our ships at sea or in port.

The knock-out blow which everyone expected has never come. Nevertheless, the sporadic attempts which the Germans have already made have provided a rich area of speculation for all students of war. Either the German air force is deliberately deceiving us, which seems unlikely, or it has been created with some incredible miscalculations.

It is true that Hitler always hoped that he would not have to fight Great Britain and therefore planned his air force on the basis of fighting his immediate neighbours. But this fact is now evident: that his fighter planes cannot reach these islands and get back, for the simple reason that they cannot carry enough petrol. The result of which is that when their bombers come they fly alone and they cannot live in the presence of British fighter planes. Losses of 25 per cent and 50 per cent are not very great numerically when an attacking formation is small, but there is nothing to suggest that the losses would be proportionately smaller if the enemy came in hundreds or in thousands. The German bomber, like the German submarine, is the prey and not the hunter. No wonder Hitler looks with lascivious eyes at Holland, which might just enable

The Riddle of the Air

him to send a fighting escort with his bombing machines.

What is the reverse side of the picture? Are we not equally handicapped? The answer to that is that we operate from France, and when our bombers cross the line into Germany the swift cavalry of the fighting machines can accompany them.

No wonder the High Command of the Germans discusses the business far into the night and to the grisly hour of dawn.

When spring comes and the factories of Canada and the U.S. have added their output to our own, we and the French may well have established as unchallengeable a superiority in the air as we have done on the sea.

How has all this come about? It is a strange story, and one that takes us back to the beginning of the Great War of 1914.

No one then had given any particular thought as to the task the aeroplane would fulfil in war. The High Command were frankly disdainful of it, and the little band of enthusiasts who were to act as pilots were looked upon with good-humoured tolerance.

In 1914 Germany and the Allies started about level in the air. Each side had small corps of military and naval aircraft, and no experience of their potentialities. Airspeeds of 70 miles an hour, a radius of action of 150 miles—much reduced by the slow speed of their climbing and an endurance of about 150 air-hours before complete overhaul, were considered high.

Yet one of these machines of ours that used to flutter somehow into the air achieved something in the first month of the Great War which proved of vital and historic importance. It brought back information from which was deduced the exposed flank and the gap left by von Kluck between his army and the sea. That information led to the battle of the Marne and the end of the Kaiser's dream to spend his Christmas in Paris.

Even then no one cared very much about the cranks with wings. Nevertheless, official indifference could not prevent the restless, irresponsible advance of science. Engines improved rapidly. Specialized designs were hurried forward. A Dutchman named Fokker achieved a revolutionary innovation with his designs.

In the early autumn of '15 the German Fokkers appeared on the Western Front. Previously, the aeroplanes had fought each other as if it was a game, with rifles or pistols. The Fokker had a fixed forward-firing machine-gun that was a quite different proposition. It gave to the Germans for the first and last time in the war a marked advantage in the air.

British and French industry leapt to meet the challenge. By the summer of 1916 the single-seater fighters (then called scouts) of the Allies were appearing in large numbers. Air superiority passed to the Allies, and although by local concentrations the Germans were from time to time able to inflict heavy losses on both the British and the French, their aircraft were, during the rest of the war, outnumbered and less effectual than ours.

From that time on there were, of course, immense strides on both sides, but Germany never again took the lead in construction. In addition, there was a

The Riddle of the Air

psychological factor. The Germans were definitely not bold war pilots.

It is no propagandist claim, but a record of fact, that the morale of the average German pilot was considerably below that of the British and Dominion airmen. If allowance be made for the fact that their more limited numbers and resources imposed upon the Germans a more economical use of their aircraft, it must also be remembered that probably 90 per cent of air fighting took place behind the German lines. A British pilot joined combat with the comforting assurance that unless he had been unlucky enough to bump into one of the few German "ace" squadrons he had only to press home his attack with sufficient vigour to have his opponents turn tail.

The Royal Flying Corps under General Trenchard adopted a persistently offensive policy. Costly though this proved, it achieved its object. The British fighters, seeking out the enemy machines behind his lines, made it difficult for his artillery and other co-operating aircraft to carry out their tasks.

Putting aside reconnaissance and actual battle in the air, there is still the consideration of the effects of bombing. It is accepted now that these results were not as great as was believed at the time. The exception perhaps was found in the industrial areas of South Germany which offered an exposed target. Munition output was seriously interfered with not only by the attacks but by the alarms which preceded the attacks.

Those whose duty it was to correlate all possible information on this subject contend that the German industrial population showed a high degree of demoralization. Whether that would apply to our own people in the same circumstances has yet to be proved. Many of us believe that the British morale would not be so readily disturbed.

In endeavouring to estimate the true part that the Air Force played in the War of 1914-18, I think it must be admitted that in spite of our superiority over the enemy it did not materially hasten the German defeat. There will be many who will disagree with that point of view. In that case, let me put it this way : although the Air Force hastened the process of retreat and would eventually have turned it into a rout, the retreat itself came with the smashing of the German Army by the infantry and artillery of the Allies.

With the end of the war the story takes a curious turn.

After the collapse of Germany in 1918 her Air Force was disbanded. For about ten years it ceased to exist, and for a further four years it was very small indeed. The importance of this gap cannot be overestimated in judging the present German Air Force. The club flying, gliding, and civil aviation that was subsidized as far as possible to evade the terms of the Peace Treaties was, of course, of some help to Goering when he was given *carte blanche* to build up a vast Air Force at maximum speed.

But during those missing fourteen years, cut to the bone as the R.A.F. was even for equipment and research, it preserved continuity. There was a steady output of skilled pilots and, more ultimately important still, of officers who, when rapid expansion did start, had the necessary training for command, staff duties, and the filling of the middle and higher ranks.

On the other hand Goering went full out, as he

was bound to do, for mass production in aircraft and pilots. His casualties were enormous, but the newspapers said nothing about them. He had to take a limited view as to the future. On the other hand, while we were hopelessly deficient in numbers, our draughtsmen were dreaming dreams and our experts were achieving the skill that only comes with endless, patient experiment. The Germans had the second greatest air force in history. We had almost nothing. But what we had was the best.

When Munich came we had done something to close the numerical gap, but we were in no position to take the air against the enemy. To our shame let the fact be admitted. Our men would have fought gallantly, and made the enemy pay a heavy price, but it is not impossible that the Germans at that time might have achieved complete domination of the air. That needs no translation. Imagination can say for itself what would have happened.

The result of Munich was an immense speeding-up of our whole war effort. The experts and the dreamers were told to give up the search for perfection and turn out actual machines instead of designs. The extent of the effort in the twelve months that followed has never been fully appreciated.

Not only did we have to train instructors, and to mobilize an army of pilots and ground mechanics, but the industrialists had to be taught the necessary skill before they could man the factories, many of them new or unfinished.

The pace quickened. Every day our strength grew greater, so that there was an overwhelming probability that by the spring of 1940 we could not only overtake

Men, Martyrs and Mountebanks

Germany in the quantity of her production but that we would far outstrip her in the quality and performance of the aeroplanes.

The supply of pilots exceeded every hope. They came from the Dominions and from the Colonies. Young men, clear-eyed and with adventure in their blood, volunteered in their thousands from Scotland, Wales, England and Ireland. Somewhere in the thrilling story of this island race the new generation had claimed its heritage of the skies.

Those of us who are in Parliament were given no rest by young fellows in our constituencies demanding the right to fly. Even their younger brothers around the ages of 14 and 15 formed units called the Air Force Cadets so that they could be trained in the theory of flying and spend their week-ends at aerodromes gazing starry-eyed at the monsters taking off into the air.

When the war came in September we were in a very different position from a year before. Yet we were not fully ready. That can be admitted now without giving comfort to the enemy. We needed those two months of September and October with their days of endless sunshine and perfect flying weather.

Aeroplane production increased unbelievably in that two months' lull. Planning was intensified and training facilities swiftly expanded. Industry was being called upon for the supreme effort of actual war production, and Hitler gave it time to find itself just as he gave our Army time to settle down in France.

In the matter of air-raid defence our measures were doubled and re-doubled.

Time is obviously of infinitely greater importance

The Riddle of the Air

to a nation turning over from a peace to a war footing than to a nation already so organized that it has gone into war of its own volition and at its own time.

The Germans had for years been working feverishly for a "zero" hour in September 1939 at latest.

Britain, clinging to hopes of peace, had remained upon a primarily peace-time basis. Had Hitler dared to hurl his whole air strength against Britain in those first days of September 1939, or even immediately after victory over Poland was assured, he must have inflicted serious damage.

He could have given us a very bad time—at the cost of heavy losses to himself, certainly, but nothing to what such an assault would now cost him.

Hitler gave the R.A.F. just that breathing-space that it needed.

Existing squadrons had time to fit in and refurbish reservists and recruits.

Much impatience has been expressed that during these opening weeks of the war the R.A.F. did not take the offensive, that it dropped pamphlets and not bombs over Germany.

It was immeasurably to our advantage that while he had the superior numbers and the good weather, Hitler did not use them, and compel us to compete.

There can be no harm in saying now that altogether apart from what propaganda value the pamphlets dropped over Germany may or may not have had, the exercise of dropping them was of immense value to the R.A.F.

Invaluable data were learned about a number of problems at negligible cost of life and material. Lessons were learned, and from them improvements carried out, that will, when the time comes, immeasurably ease the strain on us, and heighten the effect upon the Germans, of our air pressure.

Will there be a Jutland of the air? Will the two air forces of Britain and Germany some day fight it out?

If such a thing should come to pass, the deciding factor will not alone be the machines or their equipment. Victory or defeat will be brought about, as in all great battles, by the human equation.

One might contend that the German pilots have had the advantage of fighting in Poland, and many of them in Spain. Is that an advantage? In Spain they had little to compete against. They could take off on their bombing raids with the assurance that if there were no mechanical defect their chances of returning alive were excellent. So they swooped down upon the defenceless Spanish cities and had their sport without undue risk. It gave them that dangerous thing—a false confidence such as a boxer gets when in his training he punches his paid sparring partner all around the ring.

In Poland the circumstances were not quite the same. But again the Germans were able to overwhelm their opposition whenever they appeared. Actually, when the Polish airmen were able to go into action they revealed the Germans as something less than supermen. Nevertheless, swift and comparatively easy victory once more perched on the swastika banners.

No one will be so foolish as to deny the quality of courage to any race, but when these 'victorious' German pilots come against the French and British they are going to experience a disillusionment which

The Riddle of the Air

will be all the more intense because of their former easy conquests. Already the few fights that have taken place in the air must have set the grim spectre of doubt loose in the ranks of the German Air Force.

Back of it all is the human factor. Hitler Youth and Strength-through-Joy movements, though they may produce excellent 'politically reliable' cannon-fodder, cannot compete with the tens of thousands of individualistic, self-reliant and broadly educated young men in Britain and the Dominions who are straining at this moment to go into battle against the enemy.

Even Moore-Brabazon, with the fatalism that was upon him that night when he spoke, cannot suppress a thrill of pride when he looks upon his heirs and successors to-day.

Britain's cavalry of the air is ready. The steeds are swift, the riders fearless and skilful. Theirs may be the task to prepare the way for the break-through of the armies on the ground. Theirs may be the task to meet the onslaught of Germany's aerial might and battle it out over land and sea.

On the other hand, their very threat may be enough. Stranger things have happened. The war may be brought to an end because the weapons have become too deadly to use.

Chapter XIV

Gentlemen v. Goebbels

THE POLISH WAR IS ENDING AND THE Germans are taking over a village in Poland. Three of us are listening to them from London, thanks to a broadcasting-set and a clear night.

An odd conversation is going on, something between catechism and cross-examination. The participants are a German official from the Goebbels Propaganda Ministry and the local German minority in the captured Polish villages. Either they are naturally shy or singularly ill-rehearsed.

"Now, my German child. How does your family come to be here?"

"I don't know."

"Now, now. Surely. The Polish kings sent for your ancestors to raise the standard of agriculture here."

"So?"

The announcer switches on to another track.

"Do you know any German songs?"

This is better. An eager chorus of young voices screams the expected affirmative. Luckily they all know the same German songs, 'King Augustus the Saxon,' also the 'Horst Wessel.'

"But how did you learn the Horst Wessel song since the Poles would not let you know anything about the New Germany?"

That seems to beat them. The announcer starts prompting again.

Gentlemen v. Goebbels

"You listened secretly, perhaps?"
"Yes. Yes. We listened secretly."
"So you had a wireless then, a radio?"
"No. No."
"Because they forbade you to have radio?"
"Yes, they forbade us."
"The schoolmaster had a radio," piped up one voice.
"So, and you listened secretly to the schoolmaster's radio." This with the relieved air of one who has accomplished a hard task successfully.
"Herr Schoolmaster, you taught the boys about the New Germany?"
"Yes. I told them about it."
"What did you tell them?"
"I told them something of the Fuehrer. And the life of Hermann Goering so far as I knew it."
"The Fuehrer and Hermann Goering. That is very fine, Herr Schoolmaster. Now, Grandmother, what did you see of the battle?"
Grandma, who would be quite incomprehensible in any language, starts an incoherent gabble which the announcer translates for us into precise German as she goes.
"So. So. You were not frightened. Not when the aeroplanes came, Grandmother . . . the fliers."
"Yes. Yes, we were very frightened."
"Then what did you do?"
"We went away out into the fields in a cart."
"What drew the cart?"
"Horses. Horses drew the cart."
"But surely the Poles had commandeered all the horses?"

Men, Martyrs and Mountebanks

Apparently this is beyond Grandma, or perhaps the reception is fading.

"The Poles . . . took . . . the horses away," recites the announcer patiently.

"One horse drew the cart," says Grandma like a child who remembers its lesson.

"So you had one horse?"

But at this stage Grandma has broken down in tears and we hear Dr. Goebbels' man consoling her in soft tones.

"Now, now, Grandma. You need not cry. Not so, the Germans are here now." Grandma's tears flow more than ever. "We will never leave you again."

Grandma bursts into violent sobbing.

"Now, boys," cries the interlocutor, "let us sing 'King Augustus the Saxon'. . . ."

Thus the Germans worked on their people, and we listened to them doing it.

Time was when the recall of an Ambassador and the rupture of relations drew a curtain between nations at war. Twenty years ago we were grateful for any roundabout trickle of information that came through to us by way of neutral channels out of the enemy's country.

In this war there is an almost indecent intimacy between the conflicting nations. The Berlin Philharmonic gives us Beethoven and Wagner. In return for that Germany can listen to the B.B.C. programme of gramophone records, jazz, or ministers of the Crown telling why the black-out must be black, and that we must give our savings to war loan.

When Hitler spoke in the Reichstag we went along with the elected representatives of the German people.

Gentlemen v. Goebbels

It is true that we did not cheer in the same places as they did. But we have this advantage over them: we heard the Fuehrer first, inasmuch as sound takes a definite time to carry from the platform to the far end of the hall, whereas wireless reception is instantaneous.

We were at the sing-songs of the German Army around the Polish camp fires.

We listened to the 'pep' talks that the aviators and U-boat captains gave to cheer the German people.

One night Dr. Goebbels decided to appeal to our gentler emotions. One of his stations produced the Countess Zeppelin, an Englishwoman now resident in the Reich. With trembling voice she told us that she had a son at Sandhurst. She informed us that everything that had appeared in the British Press about Germany was a lie. She asked us how we could believe for a moment that it was the Germans who had sunk the *Athenia*. At the end the poor woman worked herself up to a great state of emotion. Half-choking with sobs she cried: "Friends, Englishmen, Countrymen, lend me your ears." There was a silence, and then the German announcer, who was obviously also in tears, spoke into the microphone:

"You have been hearing the Countess Zeppelin, a name familiar to many of you."

Once more the Teuton's genius for lack of tact had conquered sentiment.

The Germans were the first to grasp the potentialities of the radio as a weapon of propaganda. Broadcasting had been a means to kill opposition at home. They would now use it to undermine the will to oppose them abroad.

Men, Martyrs and Mountebanks

So punctually at certain hours on certain wavelengths, Germany broadcast items for our special benefit. It was an amazing mixture of ineptitude and skill. The Germans, so we have always been told, have no sense of humour. Well, the gentleman on the Hamburg wavelength certainly has a sense of humour. Maybe he got it over here along with that magnificent Mayfair accent. Here is an example:

"The British official account of this action says that the marks of incendiary bullets were discovered in the British plane. The inference is, of course, that we use incendiary bullets. If Mr. Churchill will go to any pilot in the Royal Air Force he will discover that every third cartridge used by the British gunners contains a tracer bullet. Let the First Lord of the Admiralty then hang up his trousers. Let a machine-gun pierce these trousers with a succession of tracer bullets. Then if the First Lord is in the trousers and his garments actually take fire we have lost the bet, and probably also lost the war. . . ."

One night he imitated the Archbishop of Canterbury. It would have won applause in any music-hall.

But although the Germans saw what might be done, they were not skilful enough to do it. Either the announcers had grown so used to dealing with Germans that they could not remember what other peoples are like, or they were all suddenly smitten with a loss of memory that made them incapable of recalling what they had said twenty-four hours before.

One evening they had documentary evidence that Mr. Churchill had ordered a submarine to sink the *Athenia,* and, therefore, had taken special care to have no Germans on board, who might prove embarrassing

Gentlemen v. Goebbels

witnesses. By the next evening they had somehow acquired proof that the *Athenia* had struck a British mine. On the following evening the evidence of German passengers, who after all seem to have been on board, definitely established the responsibility of British destroyers. We got tired, too, of being urged to ask the Admiralty where the *Ark Royal* was, night after night, when we had long ceased to worry about her.

Besides, there were odd contradictions in the German organization which amused us more than Hamburg mimicking the Archbishop. I suppose it is typical of Nazi thoroughness to select one man to translate the German news into English and to put another, selected for his accent, to read it. Anyhow, their proficiency was not equal, and the result was that we heard a man saying with a perfect English accent that "Herr Hess held an oration," when he meant Herr Hess made a speech.

It is impossible to say just why the inconsistency was so funny, but it was. In the upshot we became extremely interested in the personalities of the German announcers and quite indifferent to what they were going to say. Some of them became stock figures of fun in the first weeks of the War, like Charlie Chaplin or Harry Tate. The Zeesen gentleman was promptly dubbed 'Lord Haw-Haw.' We were all intrigued to be told that his real name was Hoffman, and that he used to teach in a school in Glasgow. Another announcer was rumoured to be Baillie Stewart, an officer who had been imprisoned in the Tower for treason. A third was an obscure member of a still obscurer British Fascist Party.

Naturally, the Germans did not have the war on the air all their own way.

Every night there were relays of news in German from France and England. There were also talks in German. Less enterprising than the enemy, we did not mimic Herr Hitler or Dr. Goebbels, though I feel sure the imitation might have been appreciated by their followers. But the fact that the Germans were sternly forbidden to listen to foreign broadcasts seems to indicate that they were not entirely ineffective.

Besides, we had a distinct advantage. Nazi Germany could muster few Englishmen to seduce us over the air, and those few were either renegades or nonentities. We, on the other hand, could draw on the expert knowledge and advice of many of the most honoured and respected German figures who, by necessity or often by choice, were living no longer in Nazi Germany.

Nor were they by any means all Jews or Socialists. One of the most interesting facts of this war has been the number of important German and Austrian public figures who were at the disposal of the Allies.

France was especially favoured in finding chinks in the enemy armour.

There was one programme especially put together for Austrians. It was compounded of news and views in a charming Vienna voice interspersed with the songs and waltzes of a vanished Austria, and the marching songs of that vanished Empire which had become treasonable under the Nazi régime.

There was, of course, one German who could be used with deadly effect. His name was Adolf Hitler. The Fuehrer possesses the weakness of forgetting

Gentlemen v. Goebbels

what he said yesterday. Unfortunately for him, his speeches are not merely on record, they are also on records. It was easy to play over Herr Hitler's bygone speeches. So while the Red Army was invading Poland, Germans could hear the well-known tones of their Leader warning them of the appalling danger implicit in the westward advance of Bolshevism.

To contrast what the Fuehrer had said even in 1938 with what the Fuehrer was saying in 1939 must, indeed, have been a nerve-wracking ordeal for the loyal Nazi who believes his Leader always to be right.

Herr Hitler himself was immensely impressed with British propaganda in 1918. He pays tribute to it in his book, and this passage happens to be one of those which he has not re-written by his actions. From the outset, the Fuehrer decided to do even better than the British in the last war. Lords Northcliffe and Beaverbrook had broken Germany's resolution with hammer blows. He would use a sledge-hammer against Britain. For it has always been a Nazi tenet that what is better must necessarily be bigger.

He overlooked the fact that the science of propaganda had changed fundamentally since 1918. The world to-day has become propaganda conscious. It has been deluged by propaganda plays, propaganda films, propaganda loud-speakers, propaganda parades. Hitler allocated immense sums to this new form of black-out. Ruthlessly and scientifically he built up his régime on the suppression of real truth and the substitution of German truth in the Press and on the radio. By this means he reduced the intellectual understanding of the Reich to adolescence. To talk to an educated German to-day about world affairs is to talk to a boy of fourteen.

It was only when Goebbels tried to extend his domain that the Nazi propaganda machine proved stupid, inept, and damaging to the German cause. German truth is not for export.

In Britain there was also a realization that propaganda had become fifty times more difficult to put over than in 1918. As it was impossible to find men fifty times more competent than Beaverbrook and Northcliffe, the Government did the opposite. They staffed an entire Ministry with people fifty times less efficient.

The story of the National Government's attempt in the years 1937 and '38 to cope with the problem of influencing world opinion is one of the mystery stories of our time.

During the years after the previous war, the nearest that we attained to a Department of Information or public enlightenment was an institution called the Travel Association. Lord Derby, that leader of difficult causes, was at its head. The hotels gave a little money to it, the Government donated some pennies left over from the Chancellor's table, and every now and then a well-meaning enthusiast sent a cheque for a fiver or so. Gallantly the Association did its best. It put English books into French libraries, and here and there you would find on the Continent an attractive poster of the Midland Hotel at Manchester as it was in Victorian times. Actually, the Association did everything it could with the limited means at its disposal.

Then there sprang up the British Council, a strange institution with Lord Eustace Percy at its head. Its purpose was to enlighten the world about Britain, to see that English was taught in Rumania or Yugo-Slavia, and to ensure that from time to time lecturers would go out and tell the Balkans of Britain's poetry and Britain's philosophy. When the Lord Eustace Percy became Chancellor of Durham University, his post as head of the British Council, which carried a salary of nothing a year, was handed over to that dynamic figure, Lord Lloyd.

Once Lord Lloyd loomed up as a man who might reach any place, no matter how exalted. As Governor of Bombay he handled things with an energy and firmness that is still spoken of with mixed feelings by those who experienced it. As High Commissioner for Egypt, his policy did not please Mr. Arthur Henderson, the then Foreign Minister, so Lord Lloyd came back to the lingering dusk of the House of Lords. But he had too much energy for it to be left unused. He took part in Churchill's India Bill revolt. He became head of the Navy League, and went up and down the country urging the strengthening of the mercantile marine against the possibility of war. Then he took over the British Council. He induced the Government to put up more money. He acquired a special building to house its staff, and for the first time the job of cultural relations took on a real liveliness.

Still there was a demand, and a growing one, for a Ministry of Information. Whereupon an odd thing happened. Sir Robert Vansittart was no longer permanent head of the Foreign Office. Instead, he had been made foreign affairs adviser to the Cabinet, which was strange, since there was already a Foreign Secretary and a permanent head at the

Foreign Office. However, he had been right at the wrong time about Abyssinia, and no doubt he had to pay for that error in timing. But he was to have something more than advising to do. Unexpectedly it was announced that he had been placed in charge of co-ordinating all forms of national publicity. The man of secrets had been appointed Chief Publiciser to Great Britain. The suave and subtle whisperer of the Foreign Office had been given a megaphone and told to use it.

Sir Robert may have co-ordinated all departments of national publicity—or he may not. No one ever knew. The secret is locked with a thousand others in his breast.

After Munich the demand for a Ministry of Information grew stronger than ever. It was obvious that American feelings towards this country were cooling. There was no suitable contact with the foreign Press. Obviously something had to be done. Once more the Government rose superbly to the occasion. A new national publicity department was announced with the information that it would be housed at the Foreign Office, and would be part of that austere organization. The head of it was Earl Perth, who had just retired after being Ambassador at Rome. But this time the job carried a salary. For many years, when he was known as Sir Eric Drummond, the new publicity chief had held the position of Controller-General to the League of Nations. Everybody gave him their confidences in the full knowledge that he would never disclose them. Once again, official favour had fallen upon a man whose every instinct was to distrust and to detest all forms of publicity. Somebody inquired what his official relation would be to Sir Robert

Gentlemen v. Goebbels

Vansittart as co-ordinator-in-chief. Somebody else asked where Lord Lloyd came in. So far as I know, the questions were given no reply. Perhaps no one knew the answer.

But there was cunning in the creation of this new Foreign Office publicity department. It was to be the nucleus of the real Ministry of Information which was to come into being the moment war was declared. From its womb the giant would spring. To ensure a successful *accouchement* Sir Samuel Hoare was chosen as midwife. He was to superintend the birth. His magic wand was to bring the flower from the seed.

September 3rd and war! The giant Ministry was revealed in all its splendid strength. The staff was huge and unusual. There were admirals, musicians, professors, curators of museums, civil servants, lawyers, ex-guardsmen, and some people who had never been anything at all. There were also a few journalists. In short, the total reached the majestic figure of 999.

As far as could be discovered, Lord Lloyd had nothing to do with it. Neither had Sir Robert Vansittart. As for Lord Perth, so far as the public was concerned he seemed to have been sunk without trace in the opening days of the war. An appointment as Minister of Information was about to be made.

The Government which had never failed to rise to the occasion before did not falter now. Ignoring every man of newspaper or propaganda experience, it asked Lord Macmillan, the estimable and much admired legal luminary, to take on the task.

After that, the deluge! The unfortunate Ministry could do nothing right. It gave newspapers permission to publish, then cancelled the permission when the presses were running. It very wisely bombarded Germany with pamphlets, and then told the foreign correspondents that the pamphlets were secret. The newspapers gave the Ministry no mercy. As there was no fighting except at sea, the whole country concentrated on the unhappy new department of national publicity.

Looking back upon it, the attacks were probably overdone. The truth is that, just as in 1914, the censorship was denounced as stupid and petulant. Newspapers which have to go to press on time lost their tempers, and published the contradictory instructions of the Ministry on their front pages.

The B.B.C. was also acting under great difficulties, and was utterly inadequate in the opening weeks of the war. It had prepared for extermination by the German Air Force, and when the extermination did not come all it could produce for our edification was an almost continuous playing of gramophone records.

Eventually there was a reshuffling of the staff of the Ministry of Information. Gradually it began to work properly though never brilliantly. The B.B.C., too, accepted the campaign of criticism without protest, and speedily brought its programmes up to a better level.

No one, however, will ever understand why the Government insisted on complete unsuitability as the one criterion for appointing its successive publicity chiefs. Yet not for the first time in the history of Great Britain its blunders have turned to triumphs.

The American public had been warned to prepare for an avalanche of British propaganda. Accordingly, it stood four-square to the wind, and braced itself for the shock. Nothing came. Nothing whatever. At the end of a fortnight the Americans, like all other neutrals, were pleading for Britain to give them some news.

In the meantime Germany was flooding the world with excellent action pictures and news reels of Prussian regiments marching into burning Polish villages, of German aeroplanes bombarding Polish cottages, of German soldiers rounding up wretched, unhappy Polish prisoners. Germany showered pictures of her overwhelming might on an America that makes a point of sympathizing with the weak.

She deluged all Hungary with photographs of ruined Warsaw which made its people loathe the Government that threatened the same fate for Budapest.

As I have said, the American continent called in vain for news of England. It was heartily sick of the news that it was getting from Germany. "Perhaps Britain had better go on doing nothing at all!" said the *Chicago Daily News*. "Hitler is her pluperfect propagandist."

Lord Macmillan is still at the head of the Ministry. He and Sir Samuel Hoare might well say : "Neutral opinion is 95 per cent in favour of Great Britain. Neutral opinion is 95 per cent against Germany. Could you really have secured a better result if you had appointed as Minister of Information a man who knew the job?"

There is a moral to all this somewhere, but it eludes me at the moment.

Chapter XV

The New Contemptibles

BRITISH EXPEDITIONARY FORCE, 1914.
British Armoured Field Force, 1939.
The same old songs again. 'Tipperary,' 'Long, Long Trail,' 'Pack Up Your Troubles.' Up over the dug-out goes the old label—'Ritz Hotel.' Only it has shifted from the Somme to the Saar. And it is the same enemy, though his line is called Siegfried instead of Hindenburg.

Yet what a contrast is there! The horses are gone, the rifles are reduced from 60 to 20 per cent. It has become an army of technicians. It is as different from its predecessors as was the Army of 1914 from that of the South African War forty years ago.

The more the British Army seems the same, the more essentially it is always altering.

It is one of the paradoxes of this peace-loving race of shopkeepers that its Army has the proudest history of any, and the longest. It has marched into Cologne and Kandahar, Pekin and Buenos Aires, Cape Town and Quebec. It broke Louis XIV and Napoleon and William II, and a lot of others who were not so well publicized.

Its first drill sergeants were Caesar's centurions. The circles of their earthworks and the scars of the roads which linked them can clearly be seen on any aerial reconnaissance. The marks of their chariot

The New Contemptibles

wheels are still graven imperishably on the Cumberland stone.

The senior unit in the Army list, the Honourable Artillery Company, instructed the officers of the trained bands in 1539. Now it instructs the officers for the Territorials who are lineal descendants of the trained bands in 1939. It lined the coast to repel the landing of the Spanish Armada. It marched out to meet the Hitler menace.

Casting back over those centuries, it is hard to say how and where the great changes came. But change was always at work. Far-reaching, deep, profound, shattering everything except the thin line of tradition.

Never was the change greater than in the years from 1914 to '39. The World War began as a contest between armies. It ended as a conflict between peoples. It forsook craftsmanship for mass production and man-power for machines. It taught the High Command things they had not dreamed of. It opened up possibilities they had never imagined.

To what use did the Committee of Imperial Defence and the War Office put their vast new experience in the post-war years?

In the view of the General Staff, Great Britain had ceased to need an Army save to police sections of the Empire. So no sound military policy was ever laid down at all. Meanwhile the politicians dictated that the premiums saved should be used for the propagation of good pacifist intentions.

The totalitarian States saw their chance here. They paid a sacrificial price for a sound military policy and left the good intentions to take care of themselves. Their system of government was admirably suited for that purpose. In five years Germany contrived to re-create her powerful military machine by regimenting her plant and her people and to supply it by turning over her locomotive workshops to building tanks.

The annual reports of the German railways from 1935 to 1939 showed an appalling increase in the number of accidents due to inadequate maintenance and the lack of replacement. But in exchange for that sacrifice Germany had acquired the equipment to go to war with a gambler's chance of reversing the verdict of 1918.

What had been happening in Britain? The tank was her outstanding contribution to military science in the war years. But successive British Governments, which allowed the theoretical study of the new weapon to go on, neglected to supply the practical means for implementing it.

The locomotive industry, which lends itself most easily to the creation of tanks, was drastically restricted. The amalgamation of railways under the 1921 Act concentrated manufacture in a few large shops, leaving the private firms to depend entirely on the export trade, so that they had a hard fight to keep going at all. Thus in the September crisis of 1938 the British Army was not only without the backing of a tank industry, it had not even a proper framework on which to build one.

There were two other essentials lacking. The flow of officers had been choked and there was no adequate corps of N.C.O.s to train the nation in arms.

After the Great War, after every great war, Britain

The New Contemptibles

cast off her uniform. The cry was 'Save.' Save everything. Save effort, save trouble, above all, for heaven's sake, save money. The catchword in those early nineteen-twenties was anti-waste. There were even anti-waste candidates for parliament. To satisfy them the Government devised a reduction all round which they called the Geddes axe, after Sir Eric Geddes, the portly executioner. The axe cut down the Army. It turned thousands of officers and N.C.O.s on to the streets with a fast disappearing gratuity in their pockets. The younger generation sat up, took notice and decided to shun a calling where employment was so uncertain. Besides, the Army was becoming unfashionable, even faintly ridiculous.

Clever young men wrote pacifist books that became the rage. The Oxford Union carried a motion, 'that this House refuses to fight for King and Country,' and many other University Unions passed a resolution in similar terms. The Labour League of Youth took the same line. In 1930 the League of Young Liberals called for Britain to disarm 'if possible in concert with other nations. Otherwise alone.' Mr. George Lansbury, then leader of the Labour Opposition advised his supporters not to join the armed forces. The Socialist Government withdrew public grants from Cadet Corps.

The honoured rector of St. Martin's-in-the-Fields, Dick Sheppard, formed a Peace Pledge Union whose members bound themselves not to fight in any circumstances. To this day they are resisting the national effort. Those were democratic days, and was not the Army built on the outmoded traditions of a faded aristocracy? So the supply of candidates for commissions from Universities and public schools dwindled to a little trickle, and recruiting sergeants found the public was not interested, even when there were more than two million unemployed. In the Territorial Force there were entire units that had no officers, and although the Honourable Artillery Company still went on, young men were appalled at the disgusting heartiness of its members.

But all this time a small devoted band of professional officers worked on. They hardly dared confess their activities when they went out to dinner. Yet even that fact was not all loss. Difficulty stimulated their ingenuity and opposition sharpened their zeal. They might not have the means to supplement their theories, but at least they could evolve them. They allocated the right proportions of a soldier's time between training in trench warfare and instruction in mobility. They realized the greater need for the use of signals, for the co-operation between troops and aircraft, for the development of Intelligence. The means to try out these theories might be lacking, but at least the High Command knew exactly what it wanted.

And the man who embodied this spirit more than anyone else was Viscount Gort, known mysteriously as 'Fat Boy.'

When the World War came, Gort was a young man with a lot of money. His income was said to exceed £20,000 a year and was of a kind not likely to diminish. Early in 1915, when he was serving in the Guards, he came back on leave. One of his many enthusiasms was to ride to hounds. He was not a particularly skilful horseman, but his zeal and courage made up for that, with the result that he was over every obstacle and up with the hounds. While on this leave he ran into a former friend of his, a naturalized German who was also a follower of the same hunt. When the outcry came against all people of German origin in 1914, this gentleman was politely asked to withdraw for the duration. All unsuspecting, Gort greeted him with great enthusiasm.

"Tell me," said the soldier, "have you had any good runs recently?"

The ex-German told him what had happened.

Gort's eyes flashed fire and that powerful chin of his came out a good half-inch.

"You come along with me," he said; "we will ride together and I would like to hear anyone who would say a word against you."

That was typical of the man who was destined to be Britain's Chief of the Army in the Field. There was always an inner tempest which would surge up in him at unexpected moments.

Half-way through the last war he had become a legendary figure. There is a tradition in the Brigade that a Guardsman can do no more than his duty. It is a magnificent tradition and one that has always inspired men and officers alike in their fiercest engagements in the line. What must this man Gort have been to be decorated three times with the D.S.O. and finally to be given the Victoria Cross?

I asked Field-Marshal Lord Cavan about him one night when we were dining together. Lord Cavan had been his Commander, and his eyes twinkled as his mind reverted to those days.

"The first thing you must say about Gort," he said, "is that he has no right to be alive. No man who has a triple D.S.O. and a V.C. should be above ground. The law of averages is completely against it. Yet Fat Boy was never reckless."

I wonder how true that is. His friends say that Gort's philosophy of warfare is simplicity itself. He had no more liking for storming a machine-gun than anyone else. He had no longing to feel the hot breath of the cannon's mouth upon his face. Or so they say. His own contention was that if an objective had to be taken, neither man nor devil nor hell's furies should stop him from doing it. My own feeling is that while he was a serious soldier he always felt the irresistible lure of danger. In normal life he never indulged in any recreation unless the element of danger was there.

When the war of 1914–18 was over, Gort, in company with the rest of our generation, looked wonderingly on the new world of peace.

"What are you going to do?" asked his friends.

"I think," said Gort, "that I would like to learn soldiering."

In its way it was an extraordinary decision. He had drained the flask of glory to its last dregs. His income was still over £20,000 a year. What could he find in pursuit of arms that would not be an anti-climax? What could he learn about soldiering that he did not know?

"My experience," he said, "has only been in the front line. That is merely one aspect of the business. I want to learn about intelligence, tactics, supplies, communications, co-ordination. It is all very well to say that an Army should be moved some place, but what about the organization behind it? I tell you soldiering is a great study and I am going to devote my life to it."

He applied for a course in the Staff College. So, in company with a few of his colleagues from the trenches, he went off to school and sat down with pencil and paper to study the profession which had brought him, already, his immortality. I wish that I could record that Gort was a model student. In the class-room or on duty he was above reproach, but once he was free his exuberant vitality and an odd quality of the *gamin* took possession of him. He formed an outlaw band called the Red Guards, composed of his particular cronies, and their exploits would have delighted Stalky himself. Then an officer turned up from Archangel and formed the White Guards, with the admirable purpose of offsetting Gort's 'Reds.'

The Mess was wrecked so often that the orderlies took it as the rule rather than the exception.

But, all the time, the serious Gort was studying with an intensity almost amounting to passion. He was acquiring a knowledge which marked him as a man who not only had a gallant past but a great future.

A few years after he was through his studies there were heartburnings in military circles. Gort had been raised to the rank of Colonel and appointed Chief Instructor of the Staff College. It was one of the plums of the Army, and it had gone to a man not yet 40 years of age. No one who had studied with him was surprised. He had made himself a tactical, as well as a practical, soldier. Some day his enthusiasm and his faith in the profession of arms would be certain to invigorate the run-down military machine of Britain.

Men, Martyrs and Mountebanks

However, the public paid no attention to the appointment. They had forgotten Gort as they had forgotten nearly all the heroes of the last war. The piping times of peace were on us. Film stars occupied our thoughts, and to satisfy our higher instincts we recited the mumbo-jumbo of collective security. What did it matter who was the head of the Staff College?

But roughly upon the gossamer fabric of Britain's pacific fantasy there fell the hammer strokes of fact. In 1935 the believers in collective security were shocked out of their dreams when the Abyssinian war showed that the Covenant of the League was useless without the arms to execute it. Then disillusion came in thunderclaps. Over the Rhineland hills, into the fair valleys of Austria where the young English pacifist had loved to take his holiday, into the cities of Czechoslovakia, poured the pernicious brown flood of Hitlerism. The free countries where a holiday was possible became sadly few. And somewhere, in every Englishman, a little voice was saying, "We may have to fight!"

There came the march into Prague. The great disillusion.

The spell was shattered. The dreams had gone. The League was just a broken inspiration. "They vanish in a night and we alone remain."

But there was a new broom at the War Office. His name was Leslie Hore-Belisha, and he was sweeping clean.

Too clean, said some.

For in December 1938 he cleared out the upper ranks of the Army and installed in their places a band of younger men.

The New Contemptibles

In the holocaust of older officers there disappeared much valuable experience and good judgment. But the public looked on with unstinted admiration. There was something attractive in the spectacle of the youngish War Minister; the product of the Oxford Union, this civilian, a Liberal and a Jew, smashing up all the reputed accumulations of War Office traditionalism.

It suited the dynamic temper of those times, the period of Transatlantic flights, of World Radio, of hot music and of Adolf Hitler.

Belisha's most sensational appointment was Lord Gort, at that time a Major-General, to be Chief of the Imperial General Staff. The newspapers looked up their clippings and with remarkable facility recalled his glory in the Field. Again, the public liked the story of how Belisha had collided with Gort while ski-ing in Switzerland. It seemed a good open-air overture to an understanding between the two men. So 'Fat Boy' moved to Whitehall and the new era began. Shortly afterwards I had to go there to see him.

Gort welcomed me with friendliness and vitality.

His shoulders are squared and his head leans back, almost giving the impression that he is going to start walking uphill. He is 53 years of age, thickset, but not corpulent. His mouth is large and would give the impression of coarseness if it were not for his eyes, which immediately arrest one's attention. They are china blue, the lightest possible shade of blue like the colour of the mountain rivers in the Austrian Tyrol. Only once before have I seen eyes like his. They belonged to Billy Bishop, the Canadian V.C. airman.

Men, Martyrs and Mountebanks

The Chief of the Imperial General Staff talked to me about many things. About the German High Command, the non-commissioned officers of the French Army and our own attenuated forces. He spoke as one who is married for ever to staff work and had given up the realm of front-line action. Yet when I left him I had the feeling that if the guns began to speak there would be a vacant desk at the War Office in Whitehall. I could not see Gort coming every morning to his office while his men were in action across the Channel.

And so it came to pass. When Hitler marched into Poland, Viscount Gort marched out of the War Office to become Commander-in-Chief in the Field. He had remained true to the profession of arms through the years that the locusts had eaten. He had lived to see his faith justified.

When Gort crossed the Channel somebody had to replace him as Chief of the Imperial General Staff. That somebody was Sir Edmund Ironside. Sir Edmund stands six feet four, except when he talks about the British Tommy. Then he is six feet six at least. There is no subject in all the world on which he will talk so fondly or so proudly as of the British private soldier. He thinks of the British Tommy as Britain's Ambassador wherever he goes, even if it is into enemy territory.

For that matter, he would not be a bad Ambassador himself. He knows sixteen languages. At least they say he does. It is hard to find anybody who can check it. He certainly knows the languages of the Near East, as he knows its countries. To him the Near East is the key to Empire. Yet it was not with the

The New Contemptibles

Near East that the public came to associate him. It was with the Far North. At the end of the last war Ironside commanded the motley force that held Archangel for nobody in particular against the Bolsheviks. It was a fruitful field in which to try out his languages. He learned to curse in every one of them. Otherwise the job was not enviable.

Allied policy in Russia was undetermined and contradictory. Ironside might have marched his army of polyglots to Petrograd if he had had the faintest idea what he was expected to do when he got there. Instead he did something that was probably even harder. He kept that little cosmopolitan force of White Russians, British, Canadians, Americans, French, Italians and Serbs in order through the tedium of an Arctic winter. That uncertain factor of their presence at the back of the Bolsheviks, with its constant threat of recreating an Eastern front, stopped Germany in the last weeks of the war from concentrating her full forces in the West as she had meant to do. For some months after the Armistice he was left there.

Then he came home. He was in charge of the Eastern Command with a headquarters that would be a schoolboy's dream. Installed at the Horse Guards, he could look out on the world's only mounted sentries that are one of the sights of London, or watch the Household Cavalry ride up in their breast-plates and horsehair plumes from Knightsbridge to relieve the Guard.

In the middle years of the Hitler régime, Ironside was in charge of London's air defences. It was typical of the England of those days that there should have been hardly any air defences for him to take charge of.

And there were even less to protect his next command. The Belisha broom swept him off to be Governor of Gibraltar. Men looked upon it as the sunset of a fine career. That post is usually the last step to honourable retirement, to a house at Cheltenham or a place near Bournemouth. In fact, it is almost retirement itself. For there is really not much you can do on the Rock. You can turn right and walk to Europa Point or you can turn left and walk to Catalan Bay. You can inspect the galleries, the cisterns and the Glacis, or go over to the neutral ground where there is a race-meeting on.

And, of course, you can always check up the number of the monkeys lest they dwindle too drastically, for tradition says that when the last monkey dies the Union Jack will cease to fly over the Rock of Gibraltar. There is not much in this to occupy an active brain in normal times.

Only this was not peace-time. The Spanish Civil War was raging over the Peninsula, and the fumes of the struggle were felt upon the Rock. The crisis of 1938 broke out while Ironside was in Gibraltar, and it fell to him to secure the place as best he could from probable attack by land and sea and air.

If the Near East is the key to Empire, Gibraltar is the key to the Near East. There was no better time and there were few better places from which to look out upon those lands through which the conquerors have passed to Empire or Destruction. Alexander the Great, Pompey, Napoleon, the men who dreamed

The New Contemptibles

the Berlin-Baghdad line. Ironside returned from Gibraltar and men began to see just why he had been sent there. It was not the overture to retirement. It was the prelude to fame. When Edmund Ironside came back it was as Inspector-General of the Forces.

Once when I dined with him he told me a story and there is no harm in making it public now.

In 1934, the second year of Hitlerism, Sir Edmund had attended the German Army manœuvres. They received him with every courtesy. They were only too glad to show him such equipment as they had then contrived.

Ironside, however, was less interested to know what was going off in German hands than to discover what was going on in German heads. That they would not show him. So on his last day he gave a supper party to four officers of the German High Command. He is himself a most abstemious man, but on this occasion he mobilized a perfect regiment of bottles so that the wine flowed generously and the guests drank deep. The deeper they drank the more silent they became, and the freer the flow of the wine the slower was the flow of the conversation. At last he gave up. As morning began to break the host rose wearily to his feet. Three of his guests rose with him; the fourth was beyond rising.

"Gentlemen, let me give you a toast," said Ironside. "Here is to peace between your country and mine."

"To peace between your country and ours!" clicked the three officers who were standing.

"That's right," said the drunken fourth as he lay back in his chair. "Quite right. *Peace for five more years.*"

Men, Martyrs and Mountebanks

That happened in 1934.

But Britain, too, began to wake up during those five years.

At Easter 1939 the Territorial Army, which ten years before could not fill its establishments, was suddenly doubled. It was a typical Hore-Belisha gamble, but it came off. Britain's youth was alert again. The pace was quickening fast.

The young men who had voted never to fight for King and Country began to meet each other in the evenings at the local Territorial Drill Hall, and Labour Pacifists were making recruiting speeches. Units were being filled by the most unlikely people. There were even uniforms at the Liberal Summer School.

And at midsummer Britain decreed conscription!

Conscription, the great incredible, the unthinkable engine of tyranny, the utter outside insult to the individual's freedom—it had come. It was on us. And Britain took it without a murmur.

With one great sigh that was almost of relief the young men walked off to register for service. In that great flood of young militiamen, the breakwater of aristocratic tradition was overrun. Clerks who had been in the Territorials sported an officer's stars, and young peers wore the private's battle dress. People did not distinguish much any more between those who had commissions and those who had not. You saw Lance-Corporals dining with their Captains and you did not bother to look again. It is true that there was a protest, but Belisha overruled that. Brothers in arms had become a fact, not a figure of speech. He actually issued an order that officers could not join

The New Contemptibles

clubs without first ascertaining that there was no ban on privates becoming members.

The most peace-minded people in the world had accepted conscription; the most civilian nation of them all had created a citizen army.

And the little band of experts who would not be discouraged could at last put their knowledge to the test. It was a profound revolution, and yet it was no revolution. The little thread of continuity that ran from Caesar's legions had, after all, withstood the great strain.

Had the Ministers been legal historians they would have known that there was no need for new laws to conscribe the nation. Unknown to almost everybody, there was still on every Briton the duty to do militia service when the country was in danger. It was the oldest law of all, the Common Law under which King Alfred's men had mustered to beat off the Danes.

The militiamen of 1939 were not military historians, nor were they legal experts. They did not know they were maintaining a 2,000-year-old tradition. They were simply young men who realized that even democracy must be defended. The magnificence of their response sent a thrill of pride in that grim testing period.

At the time I am writing these words the British Army in France has only seen the shadow warfare of the Western Front. With winter closing in on them and Hitler vainly seeking the witches' cauldron and the midnight hags for guidance, the clash of armies may not come until the spring.

When it comes, or if it comes, the glory of British

arms will fill the minds of men once more. This soldier and that will be made famous. Decorations will come to some and death to others. And few will ever think of the little group of fanatics, the soldiers who kept alive the faith and perpetuated the skill of their profession in those lean years between the German wars.

Chapter XVI

The Peace Offensive

ON FRIDAY, OCTOBER 6TH, 1939, HERR Hitler summoned the duly elected representatives of the German people to the Reichstag. The Polish war was virtually ended, thus completing the first part of the German plan.

No blows of any consequence had been struck on the Western Front. The first detachments of the British Army had been allowed to reach France without any attempt at molestation from the air. The Grand Army of the French Republic had assembled from the whole of France and moved to battle position on the Western Front without the Germany Army or Air Force making any move to hinder it.

Undoubtedly Hitler had decided that a swift peace would be easier of attainment if the battle lust was not roused between the great Powers. Therefore, when he addressed the Reichstag, and the whole world, it was expected that he would make some decisive, or at any rate plausible, peace offer. Such a move was undoubtedly in keeping with the general scheme which he had worked out.

It was, in fact, in anticipation of this that Mr. Lloyd George had taken upon himself to warn the House of Commons that it should be prepared to consider any offer made by Herr Hitler with patience and with sympathetic scrutiny.

As has already been noted, Mr. Lloyd George drew

upon himself the vials of Mr. Duff Cooper's wrath as a result.

No one resented his advice as to scrutinizing the peace terms, but in order to reinforce his point, Mr. Lloyd George had uttered ominous warnings about the combined economic and military strength of Russia and Germany. No doubt unintentionally, he contrived by this diversion to introduce a note of capitulation to circumstances. This was deeply resented.

So fierce was Mr. Duff Cooper's onslaught, so eloquent his language, so cerebral his emotion, that the House was soon full-throated against Mr. Lloyd George. Stung by its anger, and somewhat puzzled, Mr. Lloyd George intervened to try and restore his position. "I would have thought," he said, "that I am the last person with whom the word 'surrender' could be associated."

Unfortunately he failed to realize that though he holds a place absolutely unchallenged as the architect of victory in the last war, his actions since then had sadly lowered his great prestige. Often we used to feel of him that he would not live again until he died.

The House remembered how, during the tense situation when the Germans marched into the Rhineland, Mr. Lloyd George took upon himself to write an article for world-wide publication in which he made two points:

(1) That the guilt for the last war did not lie with Germany but with Austria, and that Austria only wanted a little scrap.
(2) If the staff conversations between the French and British resulted in war with Germany, not

The Peace Offensive

one British Dominion would send a corporal's guard.

Nothing could have been more calculated to strengthen Hitler's resolution at that moment than this unexpected manna from heaven. By one stroke of the pen Lloyd George wiped out the war guilt clause which he had imposed upon Germany at Versailles; and without having to refresh his pen with ink he denied the loyalty of the Dominions which had poured out their rich young blood for the cause of which he was the leader in the World War.

Perhaps some of us remembered, too, that when the German scythe of death was moving towards the fields of Austria, Mr. Lloyd George had stood up in his place in the House of Commons and said that the British Government should declare its position at that moment, that not a British soldier should be sent to the aid of Austria.

The British Parliament has a long memory, despite a deep vein of magnanimity, and perhaps the chorus that howled down Mr. Lloyd George on that day before the Reichstag speech took into account some of these previous misdeeds. Nevertheless, a spontaneous peace-following in the country was created by his speech. Many hundreds of letters reached him, just as many letters reached every M.P., urging that an honourable peace should be concluded as swiftly as possible.

It is not too much to say that as Hitler moved majestically to his place in the Reichstag there was a greater willingness to peace in Great Britain than there has been since that moment.

Men, Martyrs and Mountebanks

Like millions of other people throughout the world, I sat down by my wireless-set and prepared to listen to "the greatest German of all time." Frankly, I did not expect any novelty, because, for me, much listening has robbed the Fuehrer's methods of surprise. I had heard him on the wireless when he spoke at the Nuremberg Rally in September 1938, at the Sports Palace in Berlin, and on other occasions when he spoke his mind to a startled world.

Perhaps the word "spoke" is a mere sop to convention: it was more like some emotional actor in the Yiddish theatre playing the part of King Lear. The Fuehrer possesses no mean baritone, a gift which may well have determined him to abandon the painting of unwanted Austrian sunsets and to take up the business of political mesmerism.

Mr. Bernard Shaw once criticized an actor in a play of his because he had not a third note in his voice. That criticism would not have applied to Hitler, who is what one might call a baritone with a ringing B flat. Like all good artists, he keeps back his best effects; in every speech to which I have listened, his technique has been unaltered.

Herr Hitler knows that the tenor who sings Tristan will be remembered for his singing of the dying music in the last act, and not for the brave amorous music of the first. Therefore, Hitler starts in a low, unaccented —almost conversational—tone. Words pour out with an unbelievable rapidity, yet with almost a suggestion of boredom. He is reciting what all good Germans know: how he offered peace to this country and to that; how he offered disarmament and friendship to proud, misguided nations that would not accept his proffered hand. He had gone to them like a Messiah with a gospel of a new world, but he had been scorned by the hucksters and money-changers of the market-place.

The cheering crowds listening to him are held in leash, but long experience has taught them that their moment will come, and their ears await eagerly for the signal. And then it does come. Hitler steps back, his eyes flash fire, his voice travels almost a full octave. Like a tortured soul he cries out against the infamy of Versailles and the implacable hostility of the rich democracies. His voice does not reach B flat on the first effort but it touches G. The audience know, however, that he will give them the top note before he is finished. He is a master of the art of tightening the nerves and then letting them go on a glorious burst of unrestrained emotional eloquence.

On the particular morning that Herr Hitler spoke to the Reichstag the difficulties of his position must be recognized. His immediate audience did not matter. Marionettes can be made to dance, or left hanging dejectedly on their strings. On the other hand, the German people had to be considered very carefully. To them, Herr Hitler must appear as the all-conquering Cæsar, heroic in his moment of triumph over Poland, but ready to extend his patience and forgiveness to the nations of the West whom he was still willing to spare. Above everything else, he had to give the impression to the German people that he was ready to permit peace in the West, not that he needed peace.

There were also the neutrals. To them he wanted to pose as the saviour of Europe, the man whose patience was exhausted merely because peace had been refused to a distressed and tormented continent. Having murdered Czechoslovakia, Austria and Poland, he had to pose as the giver of life to the nations that remained.

Finally there was the supremely difficult audience of France and Britain, those relentlessly powerful democracies which had at last taken up arms. If only he could divide them, sow suspicion in their minds, break their will to war.

In *Mein Kampf* he had said that France was the eternal enemy and Britain the friend whom Germany must woo. But *Mein Kampf* was already out of date; and, after all, did he not write it in prison when he was young and inexperienced? Therefore, just as he had embraced Moscow against whom the whole of his hatred had been directed in the past, so he decided to reverse policy again and woo France while attacking Britain in his speech. Yet even then he must impeach the British more in sorrow than in anger, because from them would come the final verdict as to whether he would be able to make secure his conquest of Poland, Czechoslovakia and Austria, or whether he would have to fight for it.

With all this in mind, Hitler started in. For half an hour he spoke with a quiet rapidity as if he could not wait to get it over with. But soon the fireworks began. Never before had he introduced so many notes into his voice. Every time he uttered the word "peace"—and he did so again and again—he caressed it lovingly, reverently. Every time he spoke of Poland it was with a snarl. Not one word of pity. Not one word of regret.

The Peace Offensive

In years to come this speech will be examined closely by students of history. Perhaps no other document so exemplifies the many-sidedness of this strange and tragic figure. Even now much of his speech makes ironic reading, as these quotations will show:

"The German nation is to-day celebrating with the pealing of bells a victory which is unique in history. A country which had a population of 36,000,000 and an army composed of roughly 50 infantry and cavalry divisions opposed us. Their hopes and aims were far-reaching. It was taken as a matter of course that our German Reich would be annihilated. A week after the struggle had begun the dice had already been cast. Wherever Polish troops encountered German detachments they were repelled or beaten.

"With a dash that defied the dangers of death and with incomparable achievements in their marches, the German divisions, the air force, and the armoured troops, as well as the units of the Navy, immediately took the initiative, and it was never wrested from them for a single moment. After a fortnight, the greater part of the Polish Army was either scattered, captured or encircled. The German Army had during this period covered distances and taken areas the occupation of which would have have taken more than 14 months 25 years ago.

"Although a number of very ingenious newspaper strategists elsewhere pretended that the speed of this campaign was, nevertheless, disappointing for Germany, we know, in spite of this, that greater military achievements have hardly ever occurred in the history of war until now. It was only because of our cool prudence and our sense of responsibility that the last remnants of the Polish armies were able to hold out in Warsaw, Modlin, and in the Hela Peninsula until October 1.

Men, Martyrs and Mountebanks

"Individually the Polish soldier fought bravely at certain places, but his leaders, including the highest, were irresponsible, unscrupulous and incapable.

"Similarly, in the case of the fighting on the Hela Peninsula, I gave instructions not to sacrifice a single man without the most careful consideration. There, too, the enemy surrendered at the moment when the German attack was at last announced and put into operation.

"We are all moved by the profoundest gratitude when we think of the many unknown and nameless brave men of our German nation. We are all filled with the consciousness of the strength of our Army, which gives us quiet self-reliance. For this Army has not only proved its strength in its attacks but also by defending what it has gained. The excellent training of the individual officer and man explains the exceedingly small number of our losses, which on the whole are much below what we had believed we might expect.

"As I am now about to give you the number of our dead and wounded I ask you to rise. Although this number is scarcely 5 per cent of the total which we feared at the beginning of the campaign, we must not forget that every single man who has given his life has made the greatest possible sacrifice that a man can make for his country.

"According to the estimates of September 30, 1939, which are not likely to undergo essential changes, the number of dead in the Army, Navy, and Air Force, including officers, amounted to 10,572. The wounded numbered 30,322, and the missing 3,400."

[*It is estimated by the Allied military experts that Hitler's figures were approximately one-quarter of the actual totals. The losses among the so-called aristocratic battalions, where monarchist sympathies were known to exist, were very heavy, a*

The Peace Offensive

fact which has since created intense resentment in monarchist and wealthy circles in Germany.]

"If an identity of interests with Russia has now resulted the reason for this is not only to be found in the similarity of problems concerning these two States, but also in the identity of the views which have emerged in the two countries with regard to the shaping of their mutual relationships. Already in the speech I made at Danzig I have stated that Russia is organized according to principles which differ from the German views. Soviet Russia is Soviet Russia and National-Socialist Germany is National-Socialist Germany.

"One thing is certain: once the various régimes and different principles of nations are reciprocally respected all ground for any sort of hostile attitude disappears. A month ago I declared in the Reichstag that the conclusion of the Russo-German Non-Aggression Pact marked the turning point in the whole of Germany's foreign policy. The pact of friendship which has been signed between Germany and Soviet Russia will not only render possible peace, but a happy and permanent co-operation.

"Germany and Russia will together deprive the most dangerous parts of Europe of their threatening character; and each in its own sphere will contribute towards the welfare of the populations living there and thus help the cause of European peace. If certain circles to-day wish to read into these events, in accordance with their own needs, the defeat of Russia or of Germany, I should like to give this answer.

"The Russo-German Treaties should constitute an immense source of consolation to these worried advocates of world freedom, for these agreements show in an authentic manner that all these assumptions of Germany's aims in the direction of the Urals, Ukraine, Rumania, and so on are only an abortion of their morbid imaginations.

"In one respect, however, the resolve of Germany is unalterable—namely, to introduce on the east of our Reich peaceful, stable, and thus bearable conditions. In this respect, German interests and wishes coincide entirely with those of Soviet Russia. The two States are resolved not to permit problems to arise between them which might contain in them the seeds of internal disorders and thus also of disturbances abroad, and perhaps might even unfavourably affect the relationship between the two great Powers.

"Germany and Soviet Russia have, for this reason, agreed on a clearly marked boundary between their two spheres of interests, with the determination that each should be responsible for peace and order in its own sphere and do all in its power to prevent anything which might injure the other partner.

"I object strongly when a foreign statesman says I break my word because I have now carried out these revisions. On the contrary, I have carried out my solemn word, which I pledged to the German people, to put an end to the Versailles Treaty, and to restore its natural vital rights to a great nation.

"The extent to which I have restored these vital rights is modest. When 46,000,000 Englishmen claim the right to rule over 40,000,000 square kilometres, then it is not wrong if 82,000,000 Germans demand the right to live in 800,000 square kilometres, to cultivate their land there, and to devote themselves to their industry, and if they demand further that their colonial possessions be given back to them—possessions which were once their property, which they did not steal from anybody or conquer by war, but acquired honestly by purchase and treaties.

"Moreover, I have attempted in all the demands that I made always to obtain revision by means of negotiation, although it is true that I have always declined to submit

The Peace Offensive

Germany's vital rights as a humble petition to any sort of incompetent international body. So when I admit that Great Britain has the right to ask that her national interests be respected, at the very least the same right should be granted to National-Socialist Germany.

"I solemnly declare that these rights of ours are strictly limited. Everywhere that I saw that the national vital interests of my people were not threatened I advised the German nation to be modest and to renounce. It cannot be denied that ever since the German nation achieved recovery through National-Socialism, Germany's relations with the rest of the world have been clarified to a considerable extent. The insecurity which to-day weighs on the nations and their system of living together does not arise from Germany's demands, but from the propagandist distortions of the so-called democracies.

"It is most fortunate for mankind and by no means a misfortune that I have succeeded in abolishing peacefully and without compromising the political position of foreign statesmen at home the maddest extravagances of the Treaty of Versailles. The last revision of that treaty might have been realized by a peaceful procedure. Those who were not only displeased with the previous peaceful revisions but who, on the contrary, deplored the fact that a new Central Europe was emerging peacefully under their eyes, gradually giving all its inhabitants work and bread, are to blame for this."

After referring to "facts which cannot be removed by the scribbling of international, lying journalists," Hitler continued:

"Germany has concluded non-aggression treaties with the Baltic States. Her interests in that region are of a purely economic nature.

"Germany has never had any conflicting interests with the Nordic States, nor has she any to-day. Sweden and Norway were both offered non-aggression treaties by Germany, but they rejected them because they thought that they were not threatened in any way.

"Germany has refrained from drawing any conclusions detrimental to Denmark from the cession of German territory to Denmark under the Versailles Treaty. On the contrary, she established loyal and friendly relations with that country. We have not raised any demands for revision, but have concluded with Denmark a treaty of non-aggression. Our relations to that country are therefore aimed at an unalterably loyal and friendly collaboration.

"The New Reich has endeavoured to continue the traditional German friendship with Holland. It has neither found any existing differences with that State nor created any new ones. As soon as I took over the Government I tried immediately to create friendly relations with Belgium. I renounced any revision and any wish for revision. The Reich has raised no demands likely to be considered a threat to Belgium.

"Germany adopts the same attitude towards Switzerland. The Reich Government has never given cause for the very slightest doubt about its wishes for the loyal conduct of relations between the two countries. Moreover, Germany has never raised any complaint concerning this relationship.

"Immediately after the *Anschluss* had been carried out I informed Yugoslavia that the frontier of this State would be regarded by Germany as unalterable, and that we desired to live with her only in peace and friendship. A close and warm friendship based on the tradition of many years binds us to Hungary. Here also the frontiers are unalterable. Slovakia herself expressed a desire for Germany to help her into existence. Her independence has been recognized by the Reich and has not been infringed.

"In agreement with the Duce I brought about a change in the relations between the Reich and Italy. The frontiers between these two States have been solemnly recognized as unalterable. Every possibility of differences of interests of a territorial character has been put aside. The former enemies in the World War have become warm friends.

"But we were not content merely to make our relations normal; we went on afterwards to the conclusion of a close ideological and political Pact, which has proved itself to be a strong element in European co-operation. Above all, I have tried to take the poison out of our relations with France. In this direction I defined Germany's demands with the utmost clearness, and I have never wavered from this declaration. After France herself loyally solved the problem of the handing-back of the Saar territory, Germany had no further claims to make on France. There are no more such demands and there never will be any such demands.

"I have refrained from mentioning the problem of Alsace-Lorraine. I have accepted the decision of the year 1919 and declined sooner or later to enter into a bloody war for a question which has nothing whatever to do with Germany's vital needs, but which is capable of plunging every second generation into a dreadful war. France knows this. It is impossible for any French statesman to get up and say that I have ever made a claim on France which was incompatible with French honour or French interests.

"On the contrary, instead of demands, I have always expressed to France the wish to bury once and for all the old enmity and to allow these two nations, with their great historic past, to find their way to one another.

"No less have been my efforts for German-British

understanding and even for German-British friendship. I have always felt it to be one of the aims of my life to bring these two nations together, not only rationally, but also emotionally. If my efforts failed it was only because of the enmity on the part of British statesmen and journalists which has profoundly shocked me. These journalists and statesmen did not conceal that for reasons unexplainable to us it was their sole aim to reopen the combat against Germany at the very first opportunity.

"The less objective the reasons of these men are, the more they attempt to fake motives for their action by futile phrases and allegations. I still believe, however, that there can only be real appeasement in Europe and in the world if Germany and Britain come to an understanding. In the last instance I tried to put the relations of Germany and Russia on an amicable basis. Thanks to Stalin's same trend of thought this has succeeded.

"I have read recently in certain newspapers that any attempt at a peaceful settlement of the relations between Germany on one side, and England and France on the other, would be excluded ; that a proposal in this direction is merely proof that I am filled with anxiety and see ahead of me the collapse of Germany, and that I only make it from cowardice or with a bad conscience. If in spite of this I make known my ideas on this problem I am willing to be regarded in the eyes of these people as a coward or a desperate man. My prestige is sufficiently great to take this upon myself. Whether I really express these ideas out of anxiety or despair will be proved by the course of events.

"To-day I must deplore that people who have not seen enough war in their thirst for blood were not present where there has been war and before that were not present where there was shooting. I think it is my duty to raise my voice on other grounds, too. I believe I am speaking and answering in the names of those who com-

The Peace Offensive

prise the living substance on which the warmongers are at work in their minds.

"It certainly seems splendid when a statesman or a journalist gets up and, in glowing words, announces the necessity for setting aside the régime in another country in the name of democracy or something similar. But the carrying into effect of these glorious words is something different. Six weeks, no, a fortnight of gunfire and the war propagandists would quickly come round to another point of view. They constantly talk about necessary international happenings, but they know nothing about the military course of events. But I know better, and therefore I hold it to be my duty to speak.

"Why should there be any war in the West? For the restoration of Poland? The Poland of the Versailles Treaty will never rise again. Two of the greatest States in the world guarantee that. The final shaping of this territory, and the question of the restoration of a Polish State, are problems which cannot be settled by war in the West, but exclusively by Russia on the one side and Germany on the other. Moreover, the elimination of these two States from this area would not result in a new State coming into being in the territory in question, but only in endless chaos. The problems which have to be settled there will be settled neither at a conference table nor in editorial rooms, but by work spreading over decades.

"The ability of the Western Democracies to bring about orderly conditions has not been reasonably proved anywhere. Germany has not only restored peace and order in its protectorate of Bohemia and Moravia, but above all prepared the ground for fresh economic prosperity and for an ever closer understanding between the two nations."

[*Seven weeks later hundreds of Czech students were shot*

and the University of Prague ordered to be closed for three years.]

"Moreover, it should be recognized how senseless it would be to destroy millions of human lives and hundreds of millions of property in order to re-erect a framework which was regarded as an abortion by all who were not Poles. What otherwise, then, could be the reason for war? Has Germany made any demands to England which threaten the British Empire in any way or have placed its existence in danger?

"No; but if this war is really to be waged in order to give Germany a new régime, to smash the present rule and create a new Versailles, then millions of human beings will be sacrificed again; for neither will the German Reich break to pieces nor will a second Versailles emerge. But even if, after a war lasting three, or four, or even eight years, this should be possible, then a second Versailles would be a source of new conflicts in the future. No; this war in the West will not settle any problems at all except, perhaps, the finances of certain international war profiteers.

"As far as Germany is concerned, it can be stated that the Reich Government is prepared to make its aims in the sphere of foreign policy perfectly clear without any reservations. First of all, we want to say that we consider the Versailles Treaty extinct, and that the German Government, and with it the entire German nation, see no reason and no cause for any further revision except for the demand for such colonial possessions as are due to the Reich and correspond to it.

"This means, in the first place, the restoration of the German colonies. This request, let it be noted, is not dressed up in the form of an ultimatum backed by force.

"(2) To facilitate the exchange of productions it is

necessary to attain a new ordering of markets and a definitive regulation of currencies, thus removing step by step the obstacles to free trade.

"(3) The most important condition for the real prosperity of European and extra-European economies is the creation of an absolutely guaranteed peace and a feeling of security among all the peoples.

"This requires not only a final sanctioning of the status of Europe, but also the reduction of armaments to a reasonable and economically tolerable extent. It is also necessary to define clearly the applicability and the use of certain modern weapons capable of striking at any time into the heart of any nation and so causing a lasting feeling of insecurity.

"In my previous Reichstag speeches I have already made proposals in this direction. They were rejected. I believe, however, that the feeling of national security will not return to Europe before, by clear and valid international obligations, a clear definition of what is permitted and what not in the use of these weapons is given.

"It must be possible to define the use of gas, of submarines, and also the nature of contraband, in such a manner that the war will be deprived of its terrible character of a fight against women and children and non-combatants in general."

[*Before November was out, Hitler had launched his indiscriminate murder campaign by the laying of magnetic mines in the path of neutral shipping. Many women and children were drowned or killed outright.*]

"The maintenance of the present position in the West is unthinkable. Every day claims more victims. One day perhaps France will begin to bombard and destroy Saarbrücken, and the German artillery on its side will retaliate by laying Mulhouse in ruins. Then France will put Karlsruhe under the threat of gunfire, and Germany will do the same with Strasbourg. After that, the French artillery will bombard Freiburg, and the German artillery Colmar or Sélestat.

"Long-range guns will then be placed in position, and on both sides the destruction will spread still deeper. And, whatever the long-range guns cannot reach, the airmen will destroy, and it will be very interesting for certain international journalists and very profitable for the manufacturers of aeroplanes, arms, and munitions, but frightful for the victims.

"This war of destruction will not be limited to the Continent. It will extend far overseas. There are no longer any islands. The property of the European peoples will be blown-up by shells. The strength of the people will bleed on the battlefield, then, one day, there will again be a frontier between France and Germany, but instead of flourishing cities there will be ruins and endless cemeteries.

"It is probable that these remarks of mine will be regarded by Churchill and his friends merely as weakness or cowardice. I need not trouble myself with their opinion. I only make this declaration because I very naturally desire to spare my people sufferings. But should the views of Messrs. Churchill and his following prevail, then this declaration will be my last; we should then fight.

"Neither force of arms nor time will overcome Germany; 1918 will never be repeated in German history. The hope that our people will be destroyed is childish. Mr. Churchill may be convinced that Great Britain will win, but I do not hesitate for a second to say that Germany will win. Fate will decide who is right. Only one thing is certain. In the history of the world there have never been two victors, although often

The Peace Offensive

there have been two vanquished. This seems to me to have been the case in the last War.

"Let us hope that the peoples and their leaders who are of the same opinion will say the word of peace. Let those repulse my hand who regard war as the better solution. As Leader of the German people and Chancellor of the Reich, I can only thank God at this moment that He has so marvellously and wonderfully blessed us in our first hard struggle for our right, and pray to Him that He will guide us and all others on the right path along which not only the German people but the whole of Europe will find a new happiness and peace."

[*It was the first time, to most of his hearers, that the jailer of Pastor Niemœller had called upon God.*]

Hitler had spoken. Oddly enough, his speech roused no particular resentment and not a great deal of interest in Britain.

It had taken the British people a long time to make up their minds that Hitler could not be trusted, but having done so they could see no reason to reconsider their estimate of him. They felt that he had not opened the door to peace nor had he bolted it. And frankly, no one cared very much; even the band of zealots who had dedicated themselves to Mr. Lloyd George's unexpected leadership did not rouse themselves to any real fervour. The ranting actor of Berchtesgaden had played the part too often and the audience had become *blasé*. The anger of the British people is a fleeting quantity: it rises slowly and subsides quickly. But the boredom of the British people is an enduring and sinister thing. Britain had become bored with Hitler, just as Victor Hugo claimed that God had become tired of Napoleon.

Men, Martyrs and Mountebanks

A week later Mr. Chamberlain came down to the House to make his reply to the German leader. Westminster was crowded. The diplomats, the public, and even the peers were competing for every inch of room to hear Britain's answer. The interest was not merely in the substance of the reply but in the manner in which it would be delivered. Mr. Chamberlain, unlike the German leader, is not an actor. His personality is peculiarly transparent for a man who has risen to the supreme heights of politics. If he is concealing something, the most unobservant eye is made aware of it. If he is resentful or pleased, the whole House knows it. His words are almost always chosen with meticulous and legalistic care, for Neville Chamberlain is a serious student of language. If he has too little love of the colour and music of words, he has an almost passionate reverence for their exact meaning. At night he reads poetry before he goes to bed and finds release from the cares of the day in the lovely sonnets of Shelley and Keats. But when he prepares a speech, the poetry-loving philosopher of St. James's Park disappears and the realist business man of Birmingham takes charge.

Therefore, the House has learned to study his manner and his voice to find that personal attitude which his words do not necessarily divulge.

There was also an element of interest in the Prime Minister's personal position. Undoubtedly he had lost ground since the outbreak of war. He had failed to rouse the people with ringing oratory, nor had he contrived to give the nation that sense of vital leadership which is absolutely essential when the values of war replace those of peace. It had been left for

The Peace Offensive

Winston Churchill, in the House and on the wireless, to bring audacity and defiance to the grim task before the nation. Churchill's success had been complete, overwhelming. How would Chamberlain's speech compare with the spectacular performances of the First Lord? There were a few who thought that the very Premiership depended on it.

The moment he rose I suspected that we were going to see a new Chamberlain. There was no question at all but that the coming of war had crushed his hopes and mocked his sacrifice. There were many about him who thought he would be unable to rise to the new task of leading the nation to victory, so deeply was his soul opposed to war. They had failed to realize that the very smashing of the work of the dreams of the Peace-maker had steeled the soul of the War Premier. There across the North Sea was the man who had killed his dreams, the man whose insane vanity had led the world again to disaster. As Chamberlain began to speak we knew that we were listening to a man who loved peace with a devotion amounting to passion, but who had at last learned to hate:

"Last week, in speaking of the announcement about the Russo-German Pact, I observed that it contained a suggestion that some peace proposals were likely to be put forward, and I said if such proved to be the case we should examine them in consultation with the Governments of the Dominions and of the French Republic in the light of certain relative considerations. Since then the German Chancellor has made his speech and the consultations I referred to have taken place. I must now state the position of the British Government. Before, however, I inform the House of the results of our examination of the subject, I must ask Members to recall for a few moments the background against which his proposals appear.

"At the end of August the Government was actively engaged in correspondence with the German Government on the subject of Poland. It was evident that the situation was dangerous, but we believed that it should be possible to arrive at a solution if passions were not deliberately stimulated, and we felt quite certain that the German Government could, if they desired, influence their friends in Danzig in such a way as to bring about a relaxation of tension and so create conditions favourable to calm and sober negotiation.

"It will be remembered that in the course of this correspondence the German Chancellor expressed his wish for improved relations between our two countries as soon as the Polish question was settled, to which the British Government replied that it fully shared the wish but that everything turned on the nature and method of the settlement with Poland. We pointed out that a forcible solution would inevitably involve the fulfilment of our obligations to Poland, and we begged the German Chancellor to enter into direct discussions with the Polish Government in which the latter Government had already expressed its willingness to take part.

"As everyone knows, these efforts on the part of our Government to avoid war and the use of force were in vain. In August last the President of the United States made an appeal to Herr Hitler to settle his differences with Poland by pacific means in order to prevent war breaking out in Europe. At about the same time the King of the Belgians, the Queen of the Netherlands, His Holiness the Pope, and Signor Mussolini all tendered their good offices, but equally in vain.

"It is evident now that Herr Hitler was determined to make war on Poland, and whatever sincerity there

The Peace Offensive

may have been in his wish to come to an understanding with Great Britain it was not strong enough to induce him to postpone an attack upon a neighbour. On September 1 Herr Hitler violated the Polish frontier and invaded Poland, beating down by force of arms and machinery the resistance of the Polish nation and Army. As attested by neutral observers, Polish towns and villages were bombed and shelled into ruins, and civilians were slaughtered wholesale in contravention, at any rate in the later stages, of all the undertakings of which Herr Hitler now speaks with pride as though he had fulfilled them.

"It is after this wanton act of aggression which has cost so many Polish and German lives sacrificed to satisfy his own insistence on the use of force that the German Chancellor now puts forward his proposals.

"If there existed any expectation that in these proposals would be included some attempt to make amends for this grievous crime against humanity following so soon upon the violation of the rights of the Czechoslovak nation, it has been doomed to disappointment. The Polish State and its leaders are covered with abuse. What the fate of that part of Poland which Herr Hitler describes as the German sphere of interest is to be does not clearly emerge from his speech, but it is evident that he regards it as a matter for the consideration of Germany alone, to be settled solely in accordance with German interests. The final shaping of this territory and the question of the restoration of a Polish State are, in Herr Hitler's view, problems which cannot be settled by war in the West, but exclusively by Russia on the one side and Germany on the other.

"We must take it, then, that the proposals which the German Chancellor puts forward for the establishment of what he calls 'the certainty of European security' are to be based on recognition of his conquests and his right to do what he pleases with the conquered.

"It would be impossible for Great Britain to accept any such basis without forfeiting her honour and abandoning her claim that international disputes should be settled by discussion and not by force.

"The passages in the speech designed to give fresh assurances to Herr Hitler's neighbours I pass over, since they will know what value should be attached to them by reference to the similar assurances he has given in the past.

"It would be easy to quote sentences from his speeches in 1935, 1936, and 1938 stating in the most definite terms his determination not to annex Austria or conclude an *Anschluss* with her, not to fall upon Czechoslovakia, and not to make any further territorial claims in Europe after the Sudetenland question had been settled in September, 1938.

"Nor can we pass over Herr Hitler's radical departure from the long-professed principles of his policy and creed as instanced by the inclusion in the German Reich of many millions of Poles and Czechs in spite of his repeated professions to the contrary, and by the pact with the Soviet Union concluded after his repeated and violent denunciations of Bolshevism.

"This repeated disregard of his word and these sudden reversals of policy bring me to the fundamental difficulty in dealing with the wider proposals in the German Chancellor's speech. The plain truth is that, after our past experience, it is no longer possible to rely upon the unsupported word of the present German Government.

"It is no part of our policy to exclude from her rightful place in Europe a Germany which will live in amity and confidence with other nations. On the contrary, we believe that no effective remedy can be found for the world's ills that does not take account of the just claims

The Peace Offensive

and needs of all countries, and whenever the time may come to draw the lines of a new peace settlement the British Government would feel that the future would hold little hope unless such a settlement could be reached through the method of negotiation and agreement.

"It was not, therefore, with any vindictive purpose that we embarked on war, but simply in defence of freedom. It is not alone the freedom of the small nations that is at stake ; there is also in jeopardy the peaceful existence of Great Britain, the Dominions, India, the rest of the British Empire, France, and, indeed, of all freedom-loving countries. Whatever may be the issue of the present struggle, and in whatever way it may be brought to a conclusion, the world will not be the same world that we have known before. Looking to the future we can see that deep changes will inevitably leave their mark on every field of men's thought and action, and if humanity is to guide aright the new forces that will be in operation all nations will have their part to play.

"The Government knows all too well that in modern war between great Powers victor and vanquished must alike suffer cruel loss. But surrender to wrong-doing would spell the extinction of all hope and the annihilation of all those values of life which have, through centuries, been at once the mark and the inspiration of human progress.

"We seek no material advantage for ourselves ; we desire nothing from the German people which should offend their self-respect. We are not aiming only at victory, but rather looking beyond it to the laying of a foundation of a better international system which will mean that war is not to be the inevitable lot of every succeeding generation. I am certain that all the peoples of Europe, including the people of Germany, long for peace, a peace which will enable them to live their lives without fear and to devote their energies and their gifts to the development of their culture, the pursuit of their ideals, and the improvement of their material prosperity.

"The peace which we are determined to secure, however, must be a real and settled peace, not an uneasy truce interrupted by constant alarms and repeated threats. What stands in the way of such a peace? It is the German Government, and the German Government alone, for it is they who, by repeated acts of aggression, have robbed all Europe of tranquillity and implanted in the hearts of all their neighbours an ever-present sense of insecurity and fear.

"I would sum up the attitude of the Government as follows. Herr Hitler rejected all suggestions for peace until he had overwhelmed Poland, as he had previously overthrown Czechoslovakia. Peace conditions cannot be acceptable which begin by condoning aggression.

"The proposals in the German Chancellor's speech are vague and uncertain and contain no suggestion for righting the wrongs done to Czechoslovakia and to Poland.

"Even if Herr Hitler's proposals were more closely defined and contained suggestions to right these wrongs, it would still be necessary to ask by what practical means the German Government intend to convince the world that aggression will cease and that pledges will be kept. Past experience has shown that no reliance can be placed upon the promises of the present German Government. Accordingly, acts—not words alone—must be forthcoming before we, the British peoples, and France, our gallant and trusted ally, would be justified in ceasing to wage war to the utmost of our strength.

"Only when world confidence is restored will it be possible to find—as we would wish to do with the aid of all who show goodwill—solutions of those questions which disturb the world, which stand in the way of disarmament, retard the restoration of trade, and prevent the improvement of the well-being of the peoples.

The Peace Offensive

"There is thus a primary condition to be satisfied. Only the German Government can fulfil it. If they will not, there can, as yet, be no new or better world order of the kind for which all nations yearn.

"The issue is therefore plain. Either the German Government must give convincing proof of the sincerity of its desire for peace by definite acts and by the provision of effective guarantees of its intention to fulfil its undertakings, or we must persevere in our duty to the end. It is for Germany to make her choice."

Mr. Chamberlain had scored a triumph, the extent of which he probably himself did not appreciate.

When he had finished he remained on the Front Bench while the debate went on, but had he gone into the lobbies he would have found his followers and his opponents proclaiming his speech as one of the splendid moments of parliamentary history. In a rapidly thinning House, Chamberlain continued to sit in his place. Some of us wanted to send him a note to tell him how well he had done, but we dismissed the idea as capable of misinterpretation. If only he had broken his inflexible rule and wandered into the smoke-room, he would have realized how he had won the affection and respect of us all that day. He had spoken with force but without loss of dignity. Above all, he had spoken like a Prime Minister.

And he had spoken for England.

. . . . .

On October 24th Herr Von Ribbentrop decided to add his voice to the chorus. He chose Danzig for his platform and it was felt that Hitler would use him as a mouthpiece in order to reply to Chamberlain.

Ribbentrop was not in an enviable position. He had sworn that England would not go to war. He had mocked her people as decadent, soft, selfish and completely lacking in dynamic qualities. He had signed the peace pact in Paris and now France was at war. He had fashioned the axis as a weapon against Bolshevism with the result that the sword was broken while Bolshevism was smothering Germany in the embrace of its huge hairy arms. Only a man with a diseased vanity could have brought himself to speak at all in such circumstances. Only an audience of Nazis would have listened.

Ribbentrop is not worth quoting at length, but a few of his shriller passages must be recorded for the political student of the future. His fiercest attack was against that warmonger and cheat, Chamberlain, who had so duped the innocent Fuehrer at Munich.

"A part of the world," said Ribbentrop, "has praised the Munich conference as Mr. Chamberlain's great work in the interests of peace. Nothing could be more false than that. The British Government had promised their assistance to the Czechoslovakian Government of those days, thereby transforming into a European crisis a problem which, without Britain's interference, would have been solved overnight." (The British Government at no time promised their assistance to Czechoslovakia.)

"When at Munich at the eleventh hour Mr. Chamberlain offered his hand to a semi-reasonable solution of the problem, he partly made amends for his own mistake which had brought Europe to the brink of war. Why did he do that? The answer was given in his first speech after his return to London, when in the one hand he brought home the olive branch and in the other presented a gigantic armaments programme."

The roar of anger which greeted these words was almost loud enough to carry to those foreign correspondents who had pictured Mr. Chamberlain so assiduously as the trembling weak-willed dupe of the Fuehrer. These foreign correspondents had seen nothing but simplicity in Mr. Chamberlain's attitude at Munich. Ribbentrop saw nothing but duplicity.

"Chamberlain," he cried, "had hoped to divert Germany's thought of liberating the Sudeten Germans by threats of war, and only refrained from carrying out these threats because Britain had not yet finished her armament. Mr. Chamberlain did not go to Munich in order to prevent war but to postpone the war the British Government had decided upon.

"It is known that there had been a continuous anti-German agitation in Britain, that preparations for a coming war had been made in all directions, for instance, by organizing a Ministry of Blockade as long as two years ago. The British people who, at heart, would like to live in friendship with the German people were by all possible means of propaganda and at the demand of the British Government brought to a state of hatred and panic in regard to Germany.

"The aim of the British Government was by this means to bring Great Britain politically and diplomatically to the brink of an unbridgable gulf with Germany so that it would be possible to unleash the war against Germany at whatever moment appeared most favourable to them. This had to happen in such a way that there would be no way of retreat left open to the Government in face of its own people. This situation was brought about by Mr. Chamberlain guaranteeing Poland. That this guarantee was only an excuse is clear from the Government's declaration in the House of Commons that it was intended to be directed only against Germany. Not the inviolability of the Polish State but armed assistance against Germany was Britain's excuse."

Having succeeded in this incredible *volte-face*, Ribbentrop then decided to give his picture of the British Empire : "There is no part of the world," he cried, "where the British flag is not waving against the will of the people in question and where deeds of violence, robbery and lies do not mark the paths of British imperialism." *Even as he was uttering these words, the free peoples of the British Empire were mobilizing their men and their resources to assist the mother country.* "Stable conditions have been created in Europe. This is solely due to the Fuehrer." *The Black Guards, massed for his protection, shouted their assent.* "The injustice of Versailles has been removed." *Many of the bodies of Poland's murdered thousands still lay unburied.* "Britain is playing a dangerous game with the fate of her Empire. If the British Government persist in this policy it will go down to history as the grave-digger of the British Empire. The policy of Poland has proved that it is not good to challenge Germany. Chamberlain and his accomplices will have their eyes opened and filled with tears in due course. Fully conscious that right is on our side, and that up to the very last moment we have done our best to avoid this war, we shall see this struggle through with all our energy and strength, and at the end there can but be a great German victory."

With this final salvo Iago left the hall, wiped his feet

The Peace Offensive

of Danzig, and journeyed to Berlin to give a flattering account of his speech to the Fuehrer. If it were possible to add to the contempt which this unfortunate creature has inspired in mankind that speech would have done it . . . if it were possible. . . .

. . . . .

The unloved month of October came to an end and was succeeded by the misty melancholy of November.

Masses of German troops moved up towards the Belgian and Dutch frontiers. Thus, two countries, fearing that Hitler's patience had become exhausted, stood to their defences and wondered when the avalanche would come. The young King Leopold hurried to the Hague to see the venerable Queen Wilhelmina. Youth pooled its eagerness with the wisdom and the courage of age. The rest of Europe waited. Would there be an announcement of an alliance? Would there be an appeal to America? It was neither of these things. Instead, under the signatures of the Belgian King and the Dutch Queen there was issued a simple and moving appeal for peace. If, to some extent, one felt that the appeal had been conceived out of a deep sense of apprehension for their own countries, it did not alter the fact that once more there was a lofty attempt to remind humanity that there still existed a higher civilization :

"At this hour of anxiety for the whole world, before the war breaks out in western Europe in all its violence, we have the conviction that it is our duty once again to raise our voice.

"Some time ago the belligerent parties declared that they would not be unwilling to examine a reasonable and well-founded basis for an equitable peace.

"It seems to us that in the present circumstances it is difficult for them to come into contact in order to state their standpoints with greater precision and to bring them nearer to one another.

"As Sovereigns of two neutral States, having good relations with all their neighbours, we are ready to offer them our good offices.

"If this were agreeable to them we are disposed, by every means at our disposal that they might care to suggest to us and in a spirit of friendly understanding, to facilitate the ascertaining of the elements of an agreement to be arrived at.

"This, it seems to us, is the task we have to fulfil for the good of our people and in the interests of the whole world.

"We hope that our offer will be accepted, and that thus a first step will be taken towards the establishment of a durable peace."

The message was received in Berlin, and Paris, and in London. The King of England sent a reply couched in courteous and sincere language. The Prime Minister publicly thanked their Majesties for their intervention on behalf of peace. Herr Hitler waited, then declared that the British reply was of such a nature that further consideration was useless. But somewhere about the same time the German troops relaxed their pressure on the Dutch frontier and statements were made by the Dutch Prime Minister that it was most unfortunate that the Allied Press should have suggested that Germany ever intended to invade Holland or bring undue pressure upon her. The Dutch soldiers who had been waiting to flood their country went back to their barracks. Once more Hitler had been falsely accused, and the German wireless scorned the British for their unlimited and unscrupulous imagination.

After all, why should a concentration of German troops on the frontier of a small country suggest anything sinister? The Peace Offensive which had started with Hitler's Reichstag speech slowed down and came towards its end.

* * * * *

There was one more voice, representing no armed force, but yet the universal conscience. I refer to His Holiness Pope Pius XII who, in the late autumn of 1939, issued his first Encyclical. With it he sent a special message concerning the war to his priests:

"The hour when this Our first Encyclical reaches you is in many respects a real 'hour of darkness' in which the spirit of violence and of discord brings indescribable suffering on mankind.

"Do we need to give assurance that Our paternal heart is close to all Our children in compassionate love and especially to the afflicted, the oppressed, the persecuted?

"The nations swept into the tragic whirlpool of war are perhaps as yet only at the 'beginnings of sorrows,' but even now there reign in thousands of families death and desolation, lamentation and misery.

"The blood of countless human beings, even non-combatants, raises a piteous dirge over a nation such as Our dear Poland, which, for its fidelity to the Church, for its services in the defence of Christian civilization, written in indelible characters in the annals of history, has a right to the generous and brotherly sympathy of the whole world.

"Convinced that the use of force on one side would be answered by recourse to arms on the other, We considered it a duty inseparable from Our apostolic office and of Christian charity to try every means to spare mankind and Christianity the horrors of a world conflagration, even at the risk of having Our intentions and Our aims misunderstood. Our advice, if heard with respect, was not, however, followed, and while Our pastoral heart looks on with sorrow and foreboding, the image of the Good Shepherd comes up before Our gaze, and it seems as though We ought to repeat to the world in His name 'if thou . . . hadst known . . . the things that are to thy peace ; but now they are hidden from thy eyes.'

"The world and all those who are stricken by the calamity of the war must know that the obligation of Christian love, the very foundation of the Kingdom of Christ, is not an empty word but a living reality.

"We have full confidence that all Our sons, especially those who are not being tried by the scourge of war, will be mindful in imitation of the Divine Samaritan of all those who, as victims of the war, have a right to compassion and help.

"Whatever We can do to hasten the day when the dove of peace may find on this earth, submerged in a deluge of discord, somewhere to alight, We shall continue to do, trusting in those statesmen, who before the outbreak of war nobly toiled to avert such a scourge from the peoples ; trusting in the millions of souls of all countries and of every sphere, who call not for justice alone but for love and mercy ; above all, trust-

The Peace Offensive

ing in God Almighty to Whom We daily address the prayer: 'In the shadow of thy wings will I hope, until iniquity pass away.'

"And you, white legions of children, who are so loved and dear to Jesus, raise up your simple and innocent prayers and unite them with those of the universal Church.

"Pray, every one, pray uninterruptedly: 'Pray without ceasing.'

"In this way you will put into practice the sublime precept of the Divine Master, the most sacred testament 'that they all may be one,' that all may live in unity of faith and of love.

"In the confidence that God, 'the author and lover of peace,' will hear the supplications of the Church, We impart to you all as a pledge of the abundance of divine grace, from the fullness of Our paternal heart, the Apostolic Benediction.

"Given at Castelgandolfo, near Rome, on the twentieth day of October, in the year of Our Lord 1939, the first of Our Pontificate.

"Pius PP. XII."

I am not a Roman Catholic, but I have vivid memories of an audience with the then Cardinal Pacelli at the Vatican a fortnight or so before he was elected Pope. It was on the Friday morning of Mr. Chamberlain's visit to Rome. My audience with the Cardinal, as it happened, was on the same day that he was to receive the Prime Minister.

The Vatican was a blaze of uniforms and there was a sense of excitement everywhere at the expected visit of the British Prime Minister.

I was curious as to the personality of the Cardinal

who had for so long occupied the position of Secretary of State for foreign affairs at the Vatican. I thought perhaps that I would meet one of those politicians of the Church such as Cardinal Richelieu or Cardinal Mazarin. This Secretary of State had served in Berlin and other capitals of the world as an Apostolic diplomat. With some knowledge of the diplomatic life of Europe, I was anxious to see to what degree he would be able to blend his double responsibility to temporal and clerical affairs.

I discovered in him a man of the greatest gentleness and unassuming spirituality. Obviously he had crucified the flesh so that the spirit might reign unchallenged and unbesmirched. He talked to me in confidence but with the greatest frankness on what was going on in Spain, in Germany, and even in Italy itself. As he talked, it became evident that he was a man incapable of hatred. To him there was the one humanity which comprised all of us—men of goodwill, men of evil intent, and men who give no thoughts to the higher things of life. Again and again he spoke of the sufferings which had come not to Poland, or to Spain, or to Czechoslovakia, but *to the human family*, and his sense of pity extended even to those who were the instigators of cruelty. They, too, should be the subject of prayer as well as their victims. There was no pose about it, no intellectual compromise. It was genuine Christ-like sorrow for mankind.

When the audience was over he accompanied me to the door of his room. With a gentle and touching simplicity he raised his right hand and made the sign of the cross. "I bless you," he said, "I bless your wife and children, and I bless your country of England."

The Peace Offensive

I went out into the courtyard where the Swiss Guard were drawn up to receive the British Prime Minister in the brilliant Italian sunlight, but I felt that beyond the pageantry and unhappiness of things I had been in touch with an aristocrat of the spirit.

The universal conscience. . . .

The human family. . . .

Moving words for these times when the jungle is calling men back to the savagery from which they had merged.

Chapter XVII

Strange War

ON THE MORNING OF MONDAY, SEPTEMBER 4TH, I drove into London from Lord Kemsley's house near Stoke Poges. During the famous Sunday night we had heard the air-raid warnings given, although no one bothered very much. The war was only a few hours old, but already people were becoming veterans.

As we reached London, placards of the evening newspapers contained the news that a British liner had been torpedoed. Hurriedly we bought a newspaper. The *Athenia*, carrying a huge list of passengers, had been torpedoed with heavy loss of life on its way to Canada. Students, holiday-makers, women and girls getting away from the war zones had been the victims. Memories of the *Lusitania* came back to everyone's mind. The Hun of 1939 was not going to wait until the second year this time.

Yet there was a curious reaction. No one doubted that the ship had been sunk by a German U-boat. The attempts of the German authorities to prove otherwise were childish, and their ridiculous claims that Churchill had done it disgusted the civilized world.

But whether our emotions were so numbed by the events of the last few years, or whether we were unable to grasp the monstrousness of the thing—it failed to re-create that world-wide fury of April 1915.

There were Americans, too, on board who were

drowned, Americans who were going away from the war zones proscribed by neutrality. But even America's anger was restrained.

It is difficult to understand why.

The *Lusitania* at least was coming to these shores. There could be a suspicion, however unfounded, that she was carrying munitions for the Allies. The *Athenia* was outward bound. Even Dr. Goebbels would hardly suspect us of sending munitions from Britain to Canada.

Why did the U-boat Commander sink her? Was it an excess of zeal, or was he carrying out orders? Did he do it too soon in the war before the Germans had prepared their outcry against the blockade?

Of the many strange things that have happened in this war, the sinking of the *Athenia* will always remain something of a mystery. In its way a viler outrage than the *Lusitania*, it will be forgotten or dimly remembered when the sinking of the great Cunarder in 1915 will be spoken of as if it were but last year.

. . . . . .

Beer-cellars are jolly places. Good fellows can get together, drink heartily and sing noisily without disturbing anybody.

Sometimes beer-cellars are used for other purposes. Plotters and revolutionaries find a sense of security in the dim light and the silent barrels.

The Buergerbraeukeller of Munich is, of course a famous beer-cellar. It was from there that Hitler and his friends went out into the streets in the famous *Putsch* which ended in a hail of bullets from the Army, and

Men, Martyrs and Mountebanks

Hitler falling down so suddenly that he dislocated his shoulder. Every year Hitler goes back there and celebrates with the survivors the glorious episode of that day. He did not abandon the custom even in 1939.

In fact, he made a speech. It was not a very good speech, nor a very long one. It attacked the British with scorn and fury. His audience cheered for him to go on. The Fuehrer said that he had to leave for Berlin because his presence was demanded there. So out he went through the safe darkness of the streets to his special train. Then the time bomb exploded at the Beer-cellar. The ceiling under which he had spoken came crashing down. There were the cries of the wounded, and the silence of the dead.

The German propagandists rushed to the microphone to accuse Mr. Churchill. Monarchists, Catholics, Jews, Marxists and Brown Shirts were arrested. The pistols barked again, as in 1934.

People in Britain thought of that other gunpowder plot in the same month but many years ago. Whoever had put the bomb in the beer-cellar had failed, like Guy Fawkes, to bring about the anticipated reform.

King Carol, the King of Italy, the Queen of Holland, and the King of the Belgians sent messages of congratulation to Herr Hitler upon his escape. President Roosevelt said nothing. Mr. Cordell Hull, Secretary of State, explained with complete courtesy that his government were waiting for a report with the full facts. Not till then would the American government make up its mind whether or not it was glad that Herr Hitler had escaped.

The Great Neutral has its moments.

Strange War

General Von Fritsch succeeded General Blomberg as Commander-in-Chief of the German Army. He was a man of the highest character, a fact which he had no difficulty in proving when his enemies in the Nazi party charged him with gross immorality.

He was a soldier, not a politician; and he resented the political interference in the Army of which he was so proud.

In the Czechoslovakian crisis of 1938 he advised Hitler to be cautious. But the gamble came off and von Fritsch was dismissed.

The months passed by. As Danzig loomed on the horizon, he was taken back into the hierarchy of the German Army. He still distrusted the wisdom of the Fuehrer, and he still detested the interference of the Nazis with military affairs.

On the third Friday of the Polish war his death was announced. He had been killed while on patrol. Ex-soldiers of all nationalities raised an eyebrow. Since when did a general of high standing go on a patrol?

Von Fritsch was given a first-class funeral, but the German newspapers forgot about him with a swiftness and unanimity that would have been striking in any country but Germany. The fellow officers of the murdered General said nothing except to themselves.

His enemies whisper that when Hitler faces his doom the two ghosts that he will see will be those of Dollfuss and Von Fritsch.

. . . .

One evening in September in that last few minutes of the evening when twilight merges with dusk, H.M.S. *Courageous*, the aircraft carrier, was steaming on her course. Her normal escort was four destroyers but two had been drawn away on rescue work. The meagre details of that sinking have been published, but let me give the story as told me by a young friend of mine who was on board :

"It was a lovely evening, though rather cold. I was just getting ready for dinner when the ship was hit and I was thrown in a heap. All lights went out. The loud-speakers would not work and there was no way of signalling orders throughout the ship. Captain Makeig-Jones was on the bridge with Yeoman Signals and one or two other officers. He was a grand chap, the Captain. He weighed I should think about twenty stone. He had a queer soft voice that never changed, no matter what happened. He could tell you off or give you a week's unexpected leave and he would do both in the same voice. When the ship was struck he was thrown along the bridge until he came up against the side of it. Slowly he brought himself up to the perpendicular. 'Yeoman Signals,' he said, without a trace of excitement, 'that was a damn' fine shot !' Then he sent the officers that were on the bridge to other parts of the ship to see what they could do. He stayed where he was and none of us ever saw him again.

"The ship was on a terrible slant. It was impossible, of course, to get out any of the aeroplanes and it only became a matter of time when the *Courageous* was bound to sink. There was no panic, but some of the older men had a look of grim horror on their faces. You see, the *Courageous* had been manned pretty largely by the Reservists who had just been called up. They had come from civilian life and were out of condition.

Strange War

The nearest destroyer, I should say, was a mile away. A lot of the younger chaps who were, of course, as fit as a fiddle had jumped into the sea almost at once and were getting near the destroyer. Good luck to them, but it meant that the destroyer could not use its engines to come near us for fear the propellers would cut up the chaps in the water. So look at it any way you like, it was a mile swim for us. The question was when to go into the water. It was no use doing it too soon in case help arrived. On the other hand, we dared not leave it too late for fear of the suction of the sinking ship. The officers all went round talking to little groups of men, cheering them up and trying to give them good advice. Some of the chaps whistled and a few of them sang. It was all curiously unreal, although we knew the ship was finished. I hated to go and leave the older fellows behind, but I thought the *Courageous* was nearing its end so I slipped into the water. The most horrible part was swimming through the oil which spread all over the surface. That was ghastly. It was like a nightmare. However, I got through at last and started off for the destroyer. The water was terribly cold. I had swum, I suppose, for ten minutes when I heard shouts. I looked back and the *Courageous* was diving to the bottom. I felt the suction slowly pulling me back. Then it seemed to stop. The rest does not matter. I don't think I could have gone another hundred yards when I managed to catch hold of a crowded boat from the destroyer. Several of the lads in the boat were dead. However, here I am and let's talk about something else. I have a fortnight's leave, which is something. I am sorry, though, for those older fellows."

I looked at this young officer with his eager, smiling face and his unaffected courage.

"Don't you wish we could have peace now?" I asked for something better to say. The smile left his face.

"No, no," he said. "Let us finish the job this time."

. . . . .

In the second naval disaster there is no thrilling story to tell, although there were many cases of personal bravery. The whole country was shocked and startled when it saw the placards: "Royal Oak Sunk." We all remembered this battleship for a strange story a few years back when Bandmaster Barnacle had run foul of one of the ship's officers. Everyone had roared with laughter over the affair which reeked of Gilbert and Sullivan. And now it had been sunk with the loss of hundreds of gallant lives. Worse than that, it had been sunk in the waters of Scapa Flow. Again the sporting English paid tribute to the skill and bravery of the U-boat Commander. In 1918 the German fleet had been scuttled by its own crews in Scapa Flow and had gone shooting to the bottom. And now a German submarine had sent a British battleship to join the ghost ships underneath the waves.

What had happened? What could have happened?

There are theories of every kind. One was that the submarine had entered these sea-harbour waters before the war and had waited for its chance. Another was that it had followed a tanker in—but then could it have followed a tanker out? Mr. Churchill started an immediate enquiry and gradually the truth became known. There had been a flaw, a lack of absolute preparedness in one part of the approaches. In fact, a blockship which had been ordered reached there the day after the disaster. No one knows how the German submarine found the opening. Perhaps the information came from a member of the German secret service working as a British seaman on a trawler or a tanker. The truth may never be known unless the submarine Commander survives the war and gives us the actual story of his exploit. Should there have been a court-martial? Should some high naval officer's head have been delivered on a charger? That is the opinion of many men and officers in the fleet. They recalled the stern discipline of Jackie Fisher in 1914 when no reputation could survive in the face of blunders. They even recalled the classic story of the shooting of Admiral Byng in far-off days and the consequent improvement in the fighting qualities of the British Navy. But Churchill was forgiving, or shrewd. He decided against the court-martial. The dead were dead, the ship was gone. Seldom in the history of these islands have so many lives been lost so tragically, so uselessly.

. . . . . .

Shortly after the sinking of the *Royal Oak*, if you had looked through the windows into a certain Air Force mess you would have seen a strange sight. And if the window had been open you would have heard strange sounds.

It was in Scotland, not far from Edinburgh, and a group of flying officers were listening on the wireless to 'Lord Haw-Haw' of Zeesen. 'Lord Haw-Haw' was in his best form and was taunting Churchill and Britain with the loss of the *Royal Oak*. When he finished, the flying men sat dour and angry, muttering deep Scottish oaths such as their ancestors had used when the clans were about to attack the cursed English.

Unlike some of the Air Force squadrons, these pilots were men, not boys. Only a few weeks before they had been in civilian life although they had belonged to those enthusiastic amateurs comprising the Auxiliary Air Force, the week-end pilots who spent their Saturdays learning to fly in military formation.

In the early days of the auxiliary movement, the authorities were doubtful about its value. The officers of the R.A.F., as professionals, were not impressed. In spite of that, all over Great Britain new squadrons had to be created to accommodate the ever-increasing number of men who went straight from their offices on Saturday to the aerodromes.

When war came they were mobilized as part of the R.A.F. The amateurs joined the professionals, but they had still to prove themselves.

Day after day the Scots in this particular squadron near Edinburgh went through their various duties, accomplished short flights, sent reports in triplicate to headquarters, and at night went to bed looking longingly at the sky and wondering when the enemy would come.

One morning, with 'Lord Haw-Haw's' taunts still in their ears, the squadron started its day as usual. The leader of a section of fighters was on patrol when one of his pilots radio-telephoned to him that he had spotted a big, twin-engined enemy bomber.

There had been no air raid warning and the leader dropped to make sure of the identity of the stranger.

Strange War

It was an enemy machine all right and bedlam broke loose. The first of three relays of German bombers had arrived, making for the ships in the Firth of Forth, and with a deafening roar of engines the Scottish amateurs gave battle. My colleague in the House, Robert Boothby, watched it all from a roof in Edinburgh. "I have never seen anything like it," he told me. "Our planes were so swift they seemed to be thrown across the sky."

First one, then another, then a third enemy plane went down riddled with bullets. When the Germans got back it is believed that seven of their planes were missing. The week-end pilots and the anti-aircraft guns had done their work. Jubilantly the Scots returned to their aerodrome. Not one of their machines was missing.

As the pilots got out of the cockpits they tried to look and act as though it were a normal day's work, but in their eyes there was the same look of triumph as when their ancestors had won a bloody battle over the Sassenach.

Who were these gentlemen of the air who had inflicted such cruel punishment upon Goering's flying aces?

The leader of the section was a lawyer. With the shrewdness of his calling he had wagered a pound that he would be the first member of the squadron to bring down a German plane, and he won his money.

Another of the pilots who chased an enemy raider out to sea had been a stock-broker a month before.

Two other Scots who accounted for a bomber were a former sheep-farmer and the manager of a firm of plasterers.

Men, Martyrs and Mountebanks

That night in a hundred squadron messes of the R.A.F., the professionals toasted the flying Scots. In one day the auxiliaries had lost their amateur status.

. . . .

Strange War ! In the first three months many fine young fellows went to their deaths in aeroplanes and many fine men went down in the submarine toll of the sea. But the most persistent casualties were in the black-out at home. Every day during October eighteen people left their homes and did not return alive. No shots were fired over their graves, no casualty lists of honour appeared in the newspapers. They had died in the darkness which was to prevent an aeroplane invasion that refused to come. A wag on an omnibus called it "The Bore War". It got into the papers, and everyone agreed. Yet each night the nation looked at the stars and thought of the millions of men who at any moment might be flung into the worst hell which man's insanity has ever conceived. And in their hearts they prayed that somehow it might not come to pass.

The rain fell unceasingly. Then came the first sign of snow on the Western Front. That old devil Winter had come to have a look.

. . . .

The experts said the war would begin in the spring.

Chapter XVIII

Churchill and the Fleet

ON THE LAST WEDNESDAY IN SEPTEMBER, Mr. Winston Churchill, as First Lord of the Admiralty, rose to make a full report. We watched him with particular interest for reasons that can be easily understood.

For the last four years and longer he had been the *enfant terrible* of Westminster, the principal prosecutor, the outlaw, the advocate, the jury and the innocent spectator.

There had been times when his popularity zoomed to the stratosphere, and there had also been notable occasions when the House had treated him with something very near contempt. He was the man of climax and anti-climax. No one doubted his brilliance but there was a legend that he lacked judgment. He possessed devoted followers and a host of critics, but no enemies. Somewhere in his make-up was a basic vein of magnanimity which saved his victims from discomfiture, and himself from the consequences of his own impetuosity. He and Mr. Chamberlain had engaged in a hundred battles, and because of their physical proximity to each other in the House it had been almost a case of hand-to-hand fighting. Yet on the rare occasions that Chamberlain had dropped his cutlass, Churchill had stepped back and waited for his adversary to recover his defence. It was this

Men, Martyrs and Mountebanks

element of magnanimity which made it possible, when the war began, for the Prime Minister to take Mr. Churchill into his Cabinet without loss of face.

When Churchill first appeared on the Front Bench as a War Minister, we gave him a hearty cheer, yet for once he failed to respond to the plaudits of that audience which he values and understands more than any other. He seemed repressed and stumbled over his words in replying to routine questions. More than once, that indefatigable second-in-command, Geoffrey Shakespeare, had to prompt him as to the correct answer. It is true that Churchill had been at the Admiralty only a few days, but then we did not look upon him as an ordinary man who would take time to play himself in. Therefore, there was some shaking of heads. The old bandit who had been the terror of the mountain passes was cornered at last, and the fire in him was burning low.

"He looks older," said an Opposition Liberal with that instinct for change and decay which characterizes that bench of shadows.

When Mr. Churchill rose in his place that day, however, to make his first full war-time report, the Government Liberals, who have a quick eye for rejuvenation and opportunity, realized that he was going to do something spectacular. There was a twinkle in his eye. His head was thrust forward characteristically, like a bull watching for the matadore. He squared his shoulders a couple of times as if to make sure that his arms were free for the gestures that might come.

His first few remarks were cautious and exploratory. He was feeling his way and taking the measure

Churchill and the Fleet

of the situation, like a good boxer. Then he risked his first feint.

"It is a strange experience to me," he said with a sort of philosophical solemnity, "to sit at the Admiralty again, after a quarter of a century, and to find myself moving over the same course against the same enemy and in the same months of the year—" He paused, and a tense House waited for one of those purple phrases which would crystallize the incredibility of such an experience.

Churchill's face assumed an air of innocent perplexity. "—*the sort of thing one would hardly expect to happen*," he said.

The old master had played an unexpected trick on us. For sheer understatement it could not have been excelled. A roar swept through the House and a smile of satisfaction stretched across Mr. Churchill's face. The descendant of Marlborough, and he recognizes no other progenitor, was himself again.

For the next twenty minutes the foreign diplomats in the gallery must have wondered if, indeed, we were not a mad nation. Here was the political head of the Navy describing the grim horror of submarine warfare while shouts of laughter again and again greeted his sallies. It was not that Churchill descended to buffoonery or even to humour of an ordinary kind. The fact is that he is a great actor, and he was playing a role which he knew the House would enjoy and which it would approve. From the beginning of the war our Ministers of State had spoken in solemn uninspired language, indulging in no harsh abuse of the enemy nor exalting our own qualities beyond their proper limit. In fact the politeness of the war had induced a deep depression over Britain. Therefore Churchill decided to play the buccaneer, the gentleman adventurer back for an hour from the golden splendour of the Elizabethan Age. One felt, listening to him, that he was on the bridge of a fighting sloop in the midst of a gale ; that if he had not had a white ensign flying at the mast-head it might well have been the Jolly Roger.

One moment he would speak of the enemy with disdain, and then an inherent chivalry would make him pause.

"From time to time," he said, "the German U-boat commanders have tried their best to behave with humanity. We have seen them give good warning, and also endeavour to help the crews to find their way to port. One German captain signalled to me personally the position of a British ship that he had just sunk. He signed his message : 'German submarine.' "

Churchill extended his hands as if to ask the House to realize his predicament. Then he went on :

"I was in some doubt at the time to what address I should direct a reply. However, he is now in our hands, and is treated with all consideration."

He almost gave the impression that he had been at the detention camp to receive his gracious prisoner and had exchanged cigars with him.

Of course, Churchill had a glorious story to tell. Nothing is .more heartening than the splendid preparedness of the British Navy for the conflict that was ahead. That credit must go to the admirals who went through the laborious and thankless tasks of keeping the Navy supreme and equipped for every emergency.

Nothing had been left to chance. In seaports in all

parts of the world, guns had been stored to equip our merchantmen the moment hostilities started. In addition, there had been a steady process of strengthening the decks of these ships so that they could properly take the weight and vibration of the guns.

The bad days of Abyssinia had been left far behind. Never again would we have a fleet of shadow ships and guns that could only threaten and be unable to make good the threat. By 1938 the Naval estimates had reached the figure of 126 million pounds, It was a record for peace-time. But by the spring of 1939 the total had gone up to 149 million pounds. The House of Commons cheered the estimates, and the public approved.

The British Naval yards had managed to retain their genius for building battleships which were terrifying in their grandeur, and increasingly mysterious in their intricacy. The gun-turret of one of the new battleships weighed as much as a destroyer. Geoffrey Shakespeare explained that admirably to the House of Commons: "It is just as if we picked up three destroyers and put them on the decks of a battleship in such a way that they could be moved about like weather-vanes."

There must be something about the Navy which inspires colourful similes in those who are its spokesmen in Parliament.

Shakespeare was trying to describe to us the power of the 16-inch gun. "It is as if I went into Palace Yard where the Members' cars are parked," he said, "and picked up a car of medium size and weight and threw it with great pressure at St. Albans. And I could throw many of them in a minute."

Men, Martyrs and Mountebanks

Our minds travelled to the quiet dormitory of St. Albans 20 miles away. Then we nodded our heads with satisfaction. Experts had said the battleship was obsolete. It did not sound like it to our ears.

Mr. Churchill, before the war of 1914, prided himself on the colossal output of the British Naval yards. The average of the three years before 1914 reached no less a total than 170,000 tons. But in the years 1940 and 1941 Britain will produce fighting ships to the extent of 220,000 tons.

The achievement is a staggering one.

During that wistful period of disarmament many firms had gone out of production. Not only did our capacity for the production of Naval armaments reach its lowest level, but the skilled men drifted away and became absorbed in other industries, or, worse still, were unemployed. Inevitably the requirements of Naval equipment had become far more delicate and complicated, and the greater the demand for these qualities the less was our capacity to meet it.

When the Abyssinian crisis was over there was a nation-wide call to industry to rediscover its latent genius, and to re-create the Navy whose glory had passed. To its lasting credit let it be said that industry made a magnificent effort. There were forty factories which spent over eight million pounds of their own money modernizing their plants so as to meet the new requirements. More than any other one man, the credit of all this was due to Admiral Sir Reginald Henderson. Illness forced him to retire just as he saw the new Navy outlined against the horizon. He had courage, he had skill, he had vision and organizing capacity. The nation never heard of him. He was just another public servant who remained faithful to his dreams.

As the summer of 1939 passed its zenith, it became ominously clear the war could only be prevented by a miracle. The Navy knew that the result of that war, if it came, would depend, primarily, upon the struggle at sea. At last the conflicting theories of experts would be put to the test; and the Navy knew that so far as the sea was concerned, the war would begin on the first day and there would be no respite until peace descended once more on the troubled waste of waters.

Would the battleship be at the mercy of the aeroplane?

There were admirals who had said that the building of great ships was sheer futility. Backed by a powerful section of the Press, they contended that all our ships could do would be to get out of range and keep out of range of the enemy aircraft.

The weight of opinion, however, was against them. Those who believed in the supremacy of the battleship said: "What is an aeroplane but an instrument to propel an explosive? Unlike the gun it is not stationary. The accuracy of its aim cannot be guaranteed since it is travelling at anything from 200 to 300 miles an hour. Another factor is that its bomb, which is simply another name for a shell, must come from above, and can therefore only strike the decks, which are specially armoured. Certainly damage would be done, but it is not like a shot in the vitals of the ship. Yet even if the bomb hits us it does not compare in deadliness with a shell which in its trajectory has travelled higher than the aeroplane and which, as it comes down, has the gathering velocity of its own weight. Therefore we are struck by a missile which still has the energy of its original projection plus its own weight coming through the air."

Thus they talked, and thus they believed.

Some of their opponents asked what they would do with suicide planes where the pilot would fly his machine, loaded with high explosives, right into the ship.

To this they answered that the specially mounted anti-aircraft guns would create such a field of fire that the aeroplane as well as its pilot would have committed suicide before it reached its target.

In addition to all that there was the problem of the submarine. Admittedly science never sleeps, nor is it particular as to whom it serves.

It was known that the modern German submarine would have an infinitely greater range of activity than its predecessors of 1914. It could stay out longer from its base, it could travel distances that would enable it to refuel in different parts of the world, and its destructive capacity was greatly increased.

The British Navy was equally confident that its progress in the arts of defeating the submarine had been even more marked. Every plan had been made. Ships had been ear-marked to augment the submarine patrol. Some thousands of men from the Mercantile Marine had been trained in gunnery and sent back to their ships.

There were new devices as well.

But two things stood out from all others: one was the ability to detect the existence of the submarine by a listening device and maintain contact, the other was the new use of the air arm.

So the battle was joined. At last theories were to be subjected to the test of actual experience.

Churchill and the Fleet

At the outset it looked as if calculations had gone amiss. The submarine was going to be a far more deadly proposition than had seemed possible. The toll on our merchant ships was heavy, and there were long faces in Whitehall as well as in the suburbs. But part of the fault had been that, with splendid arrogance, the merchant captains would not wait in port for protection or convoys. They sailed out as if the sea were theirs and defied the intruder. Many brave lives were lost, and many good ships went down.

But soon the balance began to right itself. The submarine, from being the hunter became the prey. Perhaps nothing in the whole literature of horror can surpass the terrible experiences of the crews that manned the German U-boats. They might strike here, or there, but they were doomed men with only the shadow of a chance. Not only were anti-submarine ships able to locate them and send depth bombs into the belly of the sea, but the aeroplane had become an added terror. In the last war the periscope above the surface could not be seen except fairly close at hand, especially when the waves supplied an intermittent screen. Even if discovered by an alert eye and powerful binoculars the submarine could immerse itself and lead its pursuers a difficult chase.

But in this new warfare an aeroplane would come roaring full-throated across the sky. Sighting its prey, and travelling at the speed of a rocket, it would swoop down towards its victim. One by one the submarines were trapped and killed. New ones took their place. Some surrendered. But the Navy had mastered the U-boat as a decisive weapon.

With the assistance of the Germans the British

Navy was also trying out the issue of battleship v. aeroplane. Again and again British warships were attacked from the air.

At the time that I am writing these words, not a single direct hit was registered, while many planes were destroyed in the attempt.

From all this it might seem that the Navy could have sat back at the end of the third month and looked towards a period of competitive tranquillity. After all, it was not threatened by surface ships; the raiding pocket battleships were a nuisance but not more; the aeroplanes had proved, so far, to be ineffective, and the submarine was being hunted like some monster of the deep.

The Germans, though, had another and more sinister plan. Perhaps it was the 'secret weapon' that Hitler had announced in his Reichstag speech. Certainly the magnetic mine fulfilled his description that it could be used against Britain and not against Germany. There was also the parachute mine, more menacing even than the other.

On the third Saturday of November I went with Major Kermit Roosevelt to visit some friends by the seaside. This gallant son of a famous American President had come over to enlist again as he did in the last war when he won the Military Cross serving as a British officer in Mesopotamia. Having arrived at our destination Roosevelt suggested a walk in the rain. Accordingly we made our way across the fields until we came to the seashore. There was a blustering gale and the waves were brown and angry. It was a winter scene that made one want to turn back and regain the pleasant comfort of the fireside.

Churchill and the Fleet

"In my opinion," said Roosevelt, "the bravest men in the world are the crews of the merchant marine and the fishermen who go mine-sweeping in trawlers. Look at that sea. Imagine being out there, wondering what minute you would be sunk or blown to eternity or have to take to the boats."

That night there was a gale that shook the house. In the morning we read of the loss of the Simon Bolivar by striking a mine. There had been scenes of horror and a dreadful loss of life.

Other disasters were to follow with such rapidity that we realized that a grim new threat had been launched against us and that once more the minesweepers would be called to rid the sea of these metal creatures that struck at their victims when the ruffling of the water over them released their deadly power.

They are a race apart, these men who spend their whole lives in a daily battle with 'that old devil sea.' For them there is never peace. The treachery of the sea as well as its boisterous good humour is always with them. But in war-time they must face the threat of foul and cruel murder, of being cast adrift in a boat hundreds of miles from land, of chancing being rescued or lost in the lonely vastness of the ocean.

They not only have courage, they have a bravado that is magnificent.

Their names are unknown. "His Majesty's Minesweeper the ... of ... was sunk yesterday," announces the B.B.C. "Ten of her crew of seventeen were rescued."

We nod appreciatively as we look up from our books. It's good that ten were rescued. A pity about the other seven.

Men, Martyrs and Mountebanks

But at seven doors death has knocked. In seven homes children are fatherless and wives have become widows. It is more true to-day than when those haunting lines were written :

> *"For men must work and women must weep:*
> *And the sooner it's over, the sooner to sleep :*
> *And good-bye to the bar and its moaning."*

What lean years these guardians of our safety went through ! The decline of our shipping proceeded unchecked while subsidized foreign competition stole our cargoes from us. The best men in the world were left ashore to walk the weary road to the employment exchange. They asked the right to put to sea and we gave them the dole to keep them ashore.

But when the war starts it's another story. There's plenty to do when the Grand Fleet and the oldest tramps are ordered to sea together. And there's work, too, for the trawlers, every one of them.

There are big fish waiting for the trawlers. The Germans are laying mines anywhere, everywhere. Their army holds back, but the unrestricted war against unarmed neutral ships goes on with all the proud ferocity of German might.

The enemy laid over 40,000 mines in the last war. The figure is a staggering one, but it is true. They offered a greater menace than the submarines, but the British mine-sweepers conquered them as the British destroyers finally defeated the submarine. But at what a cost ! More than two hundred mine-sweeping vessels went to the bottom, victims of the very prey that they were hunting. No wonder they called it the most dangerous service of all.

And who are the men who undertake this task? They are a motley lot, but they do not know the beginning of fear. Usually the officers in command are from the Navy, specially trained in this type of warfare. There are Naval ratings, too, and petty officers distributed among the rest. Some of the smaller vessels are manned almost entirely by fishermen who know the job from the last war and have volunteered again. There is no dearth of men despite the perils and the hardships. The challenge of the sea is in their blood. Boys with the tang of the salt spray on their faces plead to be taken along. Men who have never been to sea before turn up and ask for a chance. Trawlers that a few weeks ago brought in their catch of fish have been converted into Service ships of His Majesty's Navy. Sometimes there was no market for the fish that they used to bring back, but these iron fish are in great demand.

And as in the last war the fisher folk of Newfoundland have come again to share the vigil of the seas. Their loyalty survives the hardness of their lot.

The routes must be kept clear. Come hail and tempest, come storm or calm, come sunshine, moonlight or violent death, the sea roads that lead to our island must be safe for traffic or we die.

The Army must be fed, the Air Force and the munition workers—the women and children and office workers must have their cup of tea and their morning bacon—the politicians and the air wardens must eat, and the conscientious objector cannot be left to starve.

Men, Martyrs and Mountebanks

The men who sail the seas and the men who sweep away the enemy mines are our first line of defence.

No wonder Churchill carries himself with pride and even arrogance. He is a man of action and his ships are never at rest. He is a man who is not afraid of battle and his ships are battling every hour of the day and night. The Admiralty lights burn late these nights as men chart the movements of the destroyers whose escort work and submarine-hunting give their crews no rest from the relentless winter seas that break over their decks.

The British people are proud of their Air Force and their rapidly growing Army but there is a special place in their hearts for the men of the Navy and the Mercantile Marine—and for the simple fishermen of the coastal towns who set out in their trawlers at dawn to cleanse the sea of the terror laid by U-boats that creep out at night.

Chapter XIX

Europe Yesterday, To-day and To-morrow

RARELY HAS LIFE FOR MOST MEN BEEN such an amazing compound of deep fears and high-pitched hope as it was in Europe on the eve of the War of 1939.

Old people feared to invest their savings.

Many young people were afraid to get married, while parents wondered what kind of a world their children would find.

I had a friend, a Cambridge graduate in his early twenties, who suddenly threw up his Civil Service post and withdrew to an Essex cottage.

"Have you the means to live on here without working?" I asked him.

"For just two years," he said.

"And then?"

"Then the bust-up will come and decide things for me."

His want of confidence was typical of many others. Ever since the end of the last war we had been haunted by the sense that something ominous was going to happen. It varied from time to time, of course. Sometimes we were afraid of a Communist Revolution; sometimes of being driven out of the world's markets by America, Russia or Japan. We feared French hegemony, a Communist crusade, a Revolution in India, and the Secession of South Africa. The one thing we were not afraid of until nearly the end was the thing that actually happened, a second war against Germany.

Yet it was also an age of mighty hope.

We hoped much from the League of Nations. We hoped for a classless society, the conquest of poverty and the Federal Union of all civilized peoples. Even when our economic troubles were at their worst, and the cities of Western Europe went hungry while the farms of Eastern Europe were glutted with the unsaleable surplus of their own corn, we vaguely felt that some solution of the distributing problem might plunge us at any moment into the Golden Age.

It was a destructive period. A man of 45 at the outbreak of the second World War had seen the fall of five empires and two ancient monarchies. He had witnessed the collapse of China's immemorial system; he had watched the Sultan go, and the Caliph of Islam, the Tsar of all the Russias, the ancient empire of Austria, and the upstart empire of Germany. He was at the death of a monarchy that had ruled Portugal for 300 years and another that had governed Spain for five centuries. He had seen the complete collapse of national currencies in half of Europe and watched prosperity hammered on Wall Street. He was a witness of amazing revolutions in public morals and startling economic changes that sometimes made poor men rich but more often made rich men poor and poor men destitute.

All this gave that generation a sense of instability and insecurity, of the futility of planning ahead even before the menace of the second German war took shape in the spring of 1936.

And yet it was a creative age, despite the absence of

Europe Yesterday, To-day and To-morrow

leadership in politics and the arts. The same man of 45 had watched the conquest of the air and the discovery of wireless, the finding of the North and South Poles, the flying of the Atlantic, the first motor-car and the earliest telephone, Einstein's discovery of relativity, and Freud's researches into psychology.

For the first time in a hundred years Europe had a new architecture. It was called the Functional style, and the chief features of it were the lack of all unnecessary ornament, and the maximum provision of light and air. Great windows of sheet glass and sweeping concrete balconies were its chief style, a communal style, better suited to the needs of a factory, perhaps, than a home. Therein perhaps it expressed the collectivist spirit of the age. But it did achieve triumphs in the erection of healthy airy flats at moderate prices. It gave the manual worker a sense of space and his wife a freedom from household drudgery that had so far been unheard of. In its later stages, as applied to multiple stores and provincial cinemas, it became gimcrack and ugly, and unlike the old-time cottages it did not grow old gracefully. But at its best it could be very beautiful. I have a picture in my mind still, a cameo of Berlin in 1928.

We are looking down from the gallery of a room in the 'House of German Sport.' Below us a young girl is playing a grand piano to which another is doing eurythmics. The whole outer wall is a tall bay window; outside a grass lawn stretches away to a pine forest.

That picture sums up for me the civilization of the between-wars period.

There had never been such opportunities for the

man of moderate income. For one year's wages of a postman you could travel round the world or buy a four-seater car. Small shopkeepers, mechanics, artisans, could and did travel to the Alps, the Rhine, the Lake of Lucerne and even the French Riviera in their fortnight's summer holiday. The coming of broadcasting gave miners and farm-workers their first chance to hear Beethoven's symphonies and Mozart's minuets played by the world's finest orchestras, without moving from their firesides.

New methods of transport and new refrigerating devices brought strange rich foods and fruits to us cheaply from all over the earth. You could buy a nectarine for 2d. in London in December, and for 1s. 6d. you could enjoy a good four-course meal.

In Britain, one person in twenty had his own motor-car so that he could live out in the open country and come in thirty miles to his work without difficulty or discomfort. The landscape was plastered with the bungalows of city dwellers. It had its bad side. Unplanned and shoddy buildings destroyed vast areas of the finest English country, and the coast was fringed with shabby little huts which made havoc of the beauty of England. But these were the faults of early enthusiasm. They were being brought slowly under control, and with a nation-wide campaign to "Preserve Rural England" more and more people were beginning to appreciate beauties in it that had so far escaped them. So young people went out in buses, on bicycles or afoot (there was a great craze for hiking after 1930) and their need was met by a chain of Youth Hostels all over the Downs, the Highlands and the Pennine hills. Open-air swimming-pools everywhere catered for the healthy tastes of the new generation, and the Government began to consider National Parks on the Canadian model. Crime, drunkenness and disease were rapidly sinking. The death-rate in 1930 was 1 per cent lower than in 1910, criminal convictions had fallen from 10,165 in 1913 to 7,079 in 1936. Southern England took on a new beauty from the sweep of the motor roads lined with grass verges and planted-out with clusters of trees and blossoming shrubs.

Year by year new areas of city slums were being swept away, to be replaced by the new flats in the Functional style built of bricks and concrete around open courts, grass lawns and swimming-pools.

Though I have applied these things chiefly to Britain, they were true in varying degrees of every country of Europe. Never had the standard of living been so high for so many people. Yet it happened at a time when revolution, war and financial collapse were always present somewhere on the Continent. Perhaps it was the very sense of danger that quickened our facility to create and increased our zest to enjoy. For consider what had happened to us in Britain, during these years that saw the great advances.

We lived through a civil war in Ireland, a general strike, a return to Protection after a century of Free Trade, a departure from the gold standard, and the abdication of a king.

And now let me take you out on a June evening in the London that lived through these things. It is a fine clear twilight when even the darkness turns a shade of royal blue and all London is heavy with the scent of flowers. They were everywhere, in private and public gardens, the royal parks, the window boxes on the new flats, the vases set in the window-sills. You would hardly have found an office or a workshop without a vase full of flowers.

There is a great coming and going of cars, of smooth charabancs and green-painted buses eastward to Epping Forest, westward to the Surrey hills. Bus-loads of workers, tired but happy, are coming back from the fields and woods in that 'green belt' of open country that was being saved to form a girdle all round the teeming city. Others have been out to the new park at Whipsnade in Bedfordshire where zebras and ostriches and llamas wander freely in the great paddocks, where the branches of the beech-trees are full of chattering monkeys and gaudy cockatoos, and you can wander in the woods and stroke the kangaroos. Or, if you do not want to go so far, there is the Zoo at Regent's Park. To-night the animals are floodlit and the flamingoes massed in their illuminated pool seem like some strange composition of the Russian ballet; you can see the world's most amazing garden of roses there (2,000 rose trees are in blossom), or wander into the open-air theatre where they are performing the *Midsummer Night's Dream* under a midsummer night's stars.

Or you can go out to the river winding between the lawns at Richmond, or pace the gardens of Hampton Court where you dine in the open air at the tiltyard of Henry VIII's palace. Or best perhaps of all, you can wander under the plane trees in the London streets and drink in the soft beauty of the June night

Europe Yesterday, To-day and To-morrow

and look up at the stars that are hung in the boughs while you go on breathing the scent of all the flowers.

Not one of these things lay beyond the means of the average clerk or mechanic. And the worker of London knew that and enjoyed all of them to the very utmost. I remember in particular one such night in the June of 1938, the last year before the War. A friend I was showing about London, a Spaniard, a temporary visitor from a country torn by civil war, said : "I do not think I ever saw so much beauty in an evening. Yet essentially what matters most is that you are at peace."

But we were not at peace ; that is, in anything but name. Already the shadows were creeping over us, those shadows that in one form or another we never could banish from the world between the wars.

Europe was too near and we knew that we were more than ever a part of it ; we knew that because people used to go there—thousands of them in the summer—to bathe and bask and cycle and climb mountains and eat ices in cafés and listen to music festivals.

And over on the Continent of Europe, too, you could enjoy such evenings by the river in Budapest looking over to the old floodlit fort on Gellert hill ; in Venice on St. Mark's Square, where the lights shone down on the marble pavement as on a ballroom floor ; at Salzburg in festival time, when Mozart's measured melodies tinkled through the archways of the Baroque colonnades as though for the ghosts of a vanished Austria were standing up to dance.

But we found as the years went by that there were

fewer and fewer places where you could enjoy such evenings, because the spell was being broken more and more by the knowledge that there was suffering, discreetly fenced away behind barbed wire, somewhere very near you. That on the street corners they were mounting machine-guns and the police had taken to wearing shrapnel helmets. The horror was stalking relentlessly towards us and sooner or later it must stretch out to grip us also.

And even those who did not go over to Europe began to understand what was happening there. For Europe was coming to us. Like petals driven in the path of the storm, they came, these harbingers and warnings of our destiny—the refugees.

At no time since the last war ended had England been without its refugees.

First there were the Russians : Tsarists, Liberals, Socialists, they came in hundreds, these victims of the Communist terror. They settled down in their own communities, principally in West Kensington ; opened their restaurants, their tea-shops and their garages, and with unflagging patience, undying cheerfulness, endless charm and complete incompetence, they struggled to live in a strange land. We accepted them in those early twenties as the aftermath of the last war. It did not strike us that they could be the forerunners of the next.

But now more refugees were pouring in, and still more after them.

Not since the days of the religious wars in the seventeenth century had Britain received so many of them. There were the Jews from Nazi Germany. Harmless people they seemed, mostly middle-aged, and rather fat and very frightened; lawyers, doctors, professors, rabbis, that could earn a living only with difficulty in a strange country in middle age.

We had absorbed the Russians by then. Their children were growing up as British citizens and generally we were rather glad they had come. They brought a new quality into British life, a wistful Slavonic quality, and they also brought new arts and industries, the timber trade from the Baltic, wooden toys, Russian boots. We would have been pleased also to welcome the Jews; them also we might have absorbed, for they had something to give us. They brought the fur trade, they gave us chemists and craftsmen and makers of leather goods and optical glass. But unfortunately they came in a flood and at a time when two million of our own people were unemployed, and before we could place them there were more. This time from Austria. They were not all Jews. They were Monarchists, Catholics, Democrats, everything that Hitler found unacceptable. And after the Austrians came the Spaniards, the vanquished Republicans and the exiled Basques. Then the Czechs!

It seemed there was no end to the homeless unoffending citizens of no-man's-land, the luckless fragments of the great upheaval that were blown round the Western world like the scattered dust of the island of Krakatoa after the great explosion.

Yet even in the very way the different people received the refugees you could see how far we still were from that intelligent understanding that might have saved the world after 1918. The Labour men and the Socialist Left Wing circles generally were generous in their reception of the Republican Spaniards and the Basques. They were not unfriendly to the Jews either, or the Austrians, except the Monarchist ones. But it was impossible to forget how these same people had excused and even condoned a precisely similar persecution when its victims had been Russian Whites. It was, after all, somewhat inconsistent to denounce so loudly the persecution of Jews after having been blind so long to the persecution of Christians.

Wherever the Basques were discussed you used to hear people argue that help should not be extended to these foreigners while our own unemployed went hungry. That remark was generally made by people who had no intention of doing any more for the unemployed than for the Basques. I do not recall that it ever emanated from the unemployed themselves, for pity knows no frontiers among the poor.

Do not exaggerate the importance or the extent of all this. I have only stressed the inconsistency because it typified the essential weakness in our outlook during the two vital decades between the wars. Too often our indignation was determined by the status of the victim rather than by the degree of his sufferings. We had accepted the right principles, but we were fatally lop-sided when it came to applying them.

That was true in the international field as well and it went right back to the Peace of Versailles. The framers of that Peace admitted the principle of nationality, and they were swift to apply it whenever the nationality concerned was favourable to the Allied cause.

But in their solicitude for the natural rights of Poles and Czechs, Rumanians and Serbs, they entirely overlooked the equal claims of Germans and Magyars.

Hitler inherited this one-sidedness and he carried it many degrees further. To redress the wrongs of German minority populations under the Czechs and Poles, he proceeded to subject entire populations of Czechs and Poles to the Germans. It was a fatal and a widespread want of logical thinking which prevented British Left Wing circles, genuinely horrified by this inconsistency of Herr Hitler, from recognizing it as a distortion of their own outlook; the outlook that screamed against the persecution of the Spanish Republicans while it remained unmoved by the persecution of the Russian Whites.

It was a spirit that was and that always will be fatal to Europe both socially and internationally.

"Europe," wrote the French historian, Michelet, a hundred years ago, "is like a harp. Her peoples are its strings. While any one of them is broken you will derive no harmony from the instrument."

When I first read his words twenty years ago, I thought of Germany. Actually he was writing about Poland.

. . . . .

Europe. . . .
As I have noted in my chapter on America, General Johnson described all of us over here as a pack of mad dogs. Is that the last word on Europe?

God knows Europe has had wars, endless persecution, and endless cruelty. Wars, wars, and more wars, with a new one every thirty years at least as far back as history goes.

Yet sometimes I wonder if those wars and persecutions here in Europe are not the birth pains of all that has made life worth-while for mankind. America has had few wars and she does not persecute. But America did not produce Raphael, or Shakespeare, or Mozart.

It was in Europe that they fought for a hundred years about their Faith. But that proves at least they must have had a Faith to fight for.

It was here in Europe, out of turmoil and tragedy, that Luther spoke the words that by Faith is man set free, when he nailed to the church door at Wittemberg his challenge of man to clerical authority. It was here in Europe and out of a blind war of robber barons that they made King John set his seal to those crabbed Latin sentences on Magna Charta that have given freedom to one-half of the world.

We have persecuted men for a comma and made their lives unbearable for the sake of a sentence. If we had not done that the Pilgrim Fathers would never have spread the sails of the *Mayflower* and New England might still be the home of the elk and the Indian. For the Pilgrim Fathers also were refugees. Our peoples have been steeped in class prejudice, cramped by tradition, stifled by privilege. That is why the French *sans-culottes*, groping blindly and bloodily towards the light, gave Liberty, Equality and Fraternity to a world that should be undyingly grateful.

Europe was the home of the Inquisition, of a dozen Franco-German wars, of priests and princes and crazy kings. It took a crazy king to make men first listen to Wagner. But it was in Europe, too, that men donned the insignia of the Cross to fight in the Holy Land and die gladly in the desert with the cry on their lips: "Save the Holy Sepulchre!"

The Greek philosophers and the Greek artists combined to build, from the spoils of the Persian wars, the Parthenon. It was the lustful imperialism of Rome that taught the world to make roads and to create laws. It was in Europe, and it could only have been in Europe, that King Arthur's Knights vowed their lives to the quest of the Holy Grail, just as it was in Europe that Galileo spoke his words of Faith.

It may be that neither a man nor yet a nation can find their soul unless it be through suffering. I do not know. But I believe this. If Europe should die, this old worn-out Europe with its endless hates and futile rivalries, there will never be found anything that can replace it. You will not build a civilization to make up for Europe out of the standardized prosperity and the standardized poverty of the West. No skyscraper, even if it has two hundred storeys, can replace the cathedral spires that were designed in superstition by men who believed it was God's work to slay a man who denied the earth was flat. And all the stilted wisdom of the Orient will not make good the passionate beauty of a Shakespeare who could write *Richard II* because he loved his country and loathed its enemies. If Europe should die, then so much that makes life worth living will be buried with her. If she should die, then indeed the world will realize what sometimes it forgets in its resentment—*that civilization itself is debtor to Europe.*

Chapter XX

Patience Exhausted

AS THIS BOOK COMES TO A CLOSE THE war is in its fourth month. Napoleon's fate was decided in the Last Hundred Days, the period between his escape from Elba and his defeat at Waterloo. Hitler's fate may well be decided by the First Hundred Days of this war.

Sir Nevile Henderson said to a few of us one day at a luncheon at the House of Commons that if it were not for the horror and sadness that war brings one could watch the final episodes in the lives of the Nazi leaders with the feeling that we were seeing a Greek tragedy played before our eyes. Nothing is missing to make the affinity to the theatre complete. There is even a spice of ironic comedy. Von Ribbentrop issued invitations for a huge party at his house on the night of Saturday, September 2nd. The Fuehrer was to be there and Ribbentrop was to propose the toast "The Fuehrer! To whom England has surrendered her Empire." So certain was Iago that Britain would have come to a false understanding with Hitler before then. At the last moment the party was cancelled.

The explosion in the beer-cellar, the burial of Von Fritsch, the endless conferences of Hitler and the High Command, the savage shooting of the students in Prague, the pathetic eagerness of the German Crown Prince to affirm the loyalty of his family to the Nazis, the grim joviality of Goering playing the role of Falstaff to a leader who might have been the apothecary in *Romeo and Juliet*, the Jews crouching in the shadows, women mourning for their sons and ordered to keep their words as well as their tears hidden from their neighbours. . . . Euripides never conceived a tragedy of more colour, or one which marched so relentlessly to its climax of revenge and death.

To-day there is not one of us who does not wish the end of Hitler no matter how lingering or how violent his final agonies might be. Again and again as he watched the unforgivable spectacle of a small nation daring to resist his proposals to enslave it he cried: "My patience is exhausted." Screaming that he wanted nothing but peace, and lying to the world and to himself that he had no further territorial claims, he sent his mechanized forces across first one frontier, then another, and still another.

At last he found to his indignation that the patience of Britain and France was also exhausted. No wonder, as late as the middle of August, he was saying: "If only there were someone who would give me the truth!"

Sir Nevile Henderson told us a revealing thing at that luncheon at Westminster. "Two forces were working on Hitler's brain," he said, "and since they were completely opposed to each other one would think that they would have cancelled each other out. Instead they focused and in doing so set off the spark that plunged the world into war. Ribbentrop kept assuring him that Britain was decadent and that her moneyed classes would not let her fight. The other school of thought contended that Britain was determined to fight in order to destroy Nazi Germany. To support their case they put translated copies of anti-Hitler articles from the British Press and anti-Hitler speeches in the British Parliament before the Fuehrer. Day by day they fed the flames of fear and anger which were consuming his powers of judgment. Britain would not fight; Britain was determined to fight. Which was true? At last the opposing theories merged. If Ribbentrop were right then there was no risk in going to war. If the others were right then the war had better come at once before the Allies were too strong. And so there was war."

With all the contempt that one must feel for the cunning, ranting, medicine-man of the German tribe, I still find it possible to believe that he could have been one of the great constructive figures of history, reverenced by his own people and respected by the others. Even after tricking Von Hindenburg, even after his vile murder of Dollfuss and the bloody purge of his own followers, he could have changed from a policy of ruthless violence to one of statesmanlike responsibility. It was not too late.

When at last he is dead either by his own hand or what is legally known as an act of God, a gravestone should be erected by those who still believe in the Hitler Legend. On it there might appear the words:

> Here lies
> ADOLF HITLER
> Who died at
> MUNICH
> in September, 1938

Patience Exhausted

With some knowledge of Hitler's character I find it difficult to understand why he did not seize the place in history which was opened to him by the three keys of Berchtesgaden, Godesberg and Munich. His diplomatic victory was complete. At the point of the pistol he had demanded the Sudetenland while the victors of 1918 had been forced to stand aside.

Surely the indifferent painter of Viennese sunsets must have seen the magnitude of his own position when the Prime Ministers of Britain and France and the Dictator of Italy came to his conference table while Versailles was re-written at his command.

If he had had one touch of real greatness in him a new chapter in the history of mankind could have begun that day. But greatness demands magnanimity, a simplicity of the spirit and a recognition that there is a duty to humanity as well as to the State.

He could have said to the world: "I have pursued a violent course because my people have suffered from a cruel and unjust peace. Now Germany faces a new life without bitterness and without enmity. I shall begin a process of disarmament at once and Germany will play her full part in furthering the prosperity of the free peoples of Europe whose liberty I promise to respect and to strengthen with the years. I ask for the friendship and the confidence of the people of Britain and France. As evidence of my deep sincerity I shall order work to stop at once on the Western defences which we have been preparing. Germany asks for nothing but the respect and the co-operation of other nations in building a new and happier Europe."

Men, Martyrs and Mountebanks

One can imagine how that would have been received in Britain and America. Even in France there would have been a strong move to take him at his word. America would have offered him loans and Britain would have given him credits. Once he had restored the Jews to full citizenship again he could have crossed to New York and been pelted by joyous ticker-tape ribbons from thousands of friendly office windows. He could have come to London and we would have given him a gala night at Covent Garden and allowed him to hear a debate in the House of Commons.

Economically the position of Germany would have improved rapidly once the first shock of the change-over of industry from a war to a peace basis had been absorbed. The markets of Europe are the natural dominions of German trade. As soon as the threat of political domination was removed the tactical position of Germany, as the great importer of foodstuffs and raw materials and the dominant producer of manufactured goods, would have become evident to all. Britain's dominions are over the seas. Germany's were at her door.

Why didn't Hitler see all this? Why did he not tell Ribbentrop to be silent as the former champagne salesman gloated over the humiliation of Britain? I suppose the truth is that having lied and tricked his way to power Hitler was afraid to throw away the weapons which had served him so well. Or perhaps he felt his own incapacities as a constructive statesman who would have to balance his budget instead of shrieking slogans to his mesmerized legions at Nuremberg.

I still think that in the four days' debate at West-

Patience Exhausted

minster that followed Mr. Chamberlain's return from Munich it was a mistake for Churchill, Eden, Duff Cooper and Attlee to denounce Hitler as a sadist, a footpad, a highwayman and a gangster. They just refused to believe that the crook was going straight and they said so. There would have been no risk in giving the miracle a week or so to work.

Bernard Shaw tries to prove in *Pygmalion* that the difference between a duchess and a flower girl is the way one treats her. Hitler's enemies in Britain had no intention of trying out that theory. He had lied, he had murdered and he had blackmailed. There was no place for him in the international club of decent fellows.

Perhaps they were right. The forces that Hitler had created may have become his master. It is the story of all such things that the violence of one man leads a revolution and that in the end he becomes its prisoner. Still, I do not see what advantage there was in branding Hitler with the scarlet letter at the very moment that he had vowed eternal peace with Britain on the white purity of a slip of paper. A little delay would not have mattered.

The fates gathered the threads of destiny together. The days of peace were numbered.

And as the bells rang out to proclaim the New Year of 1939 Hitler became conscious of something which must have troubled his soul. Chamberlain, the emissary of peace who had descended into Germany from the clouds in a black jacket and striped trousers, was speaking with a growing firmness. There was every evidence, too, that Britain was rearming at an ever-increasing pace.

Men, Martyrs and Mountebanks

What had really happened between Chamberlain and Hitler at Munich?

The events of that tempestuous episode can now be seen with a clarity that rises above the mists of prejudice. Chamberlain prevented Hitler from embarking on a war that might well have proved disastrous to the Allies. Chamberlain signed the peace compact with Hitler on the thousand-to-one chance that it might work. Having prevented the war, having taken a gamble for real peace, the British Prime Minister then demanded the insurance of British rearmament on a vast scale. It would seem evident that he backed his judgment three ways.

What did Chamberlain think of Hitler? It is no secret that the Englishman looked upon the Fuehrer with contempt. Nothing is more false than to imagine that the Hitler spell worked its magic on the man from Birmingham.

But the British Prime Minister so longed for peace and so abhorred war that he kept his patience in spite of world-wide attacks that spared him nothing. They hurt him, but it only increased the quality of toughness that is his strongest characteristic. He kept his goal clearly before him—peace, if possible, or war held-off until we were ready. There are many of us who believe that no other man could have brought us into war with such national unity, such strength and so favourable a diplomatic situation. History will appraise his Premiership in the calm detachment of the years. Those who were part of it all, however insignificant, can but state their views and pass on.

War is a blasphemy against God. Yet it brings

out qualities in a race which are too often dormant in peace-time.

Look at this island of Britain to-day. The workers have risen like one man to defend their country and to strike at aggression. What can be more moving than the sight of those who have had so little from life ready to give their lives to protect the community at large? Perhaps something is in their blood akin to that of the Irish parliamentary rebel, Tom Kettle, who went out in 1914 and was killed. Grandly he wrote:

> Know then: we fools, now with the foolish dead,
> Fought not for flag or king or emperor,
> But for a dream, born in a herdsman's shed,
> And for the secret scripture of the poor.

If we rightly praise the poor or give tribute to the workers of the nation, who can deny praise and tribute to those more fortunate ones who are heirs to wealth, position and tradition?

They have seen the Chancellor come down to the House and raise the impost of direct taxation until private fortunes shrink to nothing. In every country house and in every castle the ghost of the Chancellor walks with bony finger upraised as he whispers: "Pay up, look alive, pay up. And if you dare to die, this place will be sold to meet the duties that I shall exact from your heirs. You are marked for destruction. Look on me, the banker of death. Pay, pay, pay, and hug the fire close, for the wind is raw."

The sons of the old families have not waited to be called up. They have put on uniform as naturally as they would change for dinner after a game of golf.

Men, Martyrs and Mountebanks

They have joined the crack regiments, it is true, but they know that if the battle comes the Brigade is always for it.

It is no mean thing to have lived to see this peace-loving country throw off its sloth, discard its false dreams and answer to the challenge of destiny once more. Britain is awake to-day. She is vibrant with life and ready once more to follow her star.

At long last—her patience is exhausted. Hitler's doom is written in those words.